D0844138

Immigrant Mothers

Immigrant Mothers

Narratives of Race and Maternity, 1890–1925

Katrina Irving

DISCARDED
UNIVERSITY OF TULSA LIBRARY

UNIVERSITY OF ILLINOIS PRESS

URBANA AND CHICAGO

UNIVERSITY OF TULSA-McFARLIN LIBRARY

© 2000 by the Board of Trustees of the University of Illinois
All rights reserved
Manufactured in the United States of America

∞ This book is printed on acid-free paper.

Library of Congress Cataloging-in-Publication Data
Irving, Katrina.
Immigrant mothers : narratives of race and maternity, 1890–1925 /
Katrina Irving.
p. cm.
Includes bibliographical references and index.
ISBN 0-252-02534-2 (cloth : alk. paper)
1. Women immigrants—United States—Public opinion—History.
2. Mothers—United States—Public opinion—History. 3. Xenopho-
bia—United States—History. 4. Immigrants in literature—History.
5. United States—Emigration and immigration—Public opinion—
History. 6. United States—Ethnic relations—History. I. Title.
HQ1419.I75   2000
305.48'9691—dc21   99-6616
CIP

C 5 4 3 2 1

HQ 1419
.I15
2000

For Cath Irving

I shot an arrow into the Air
It fell to earth, I know not where.
—William Wadsworth Longfellow

Contents

Acknowledgments

It's a great pleasure to be able to thank those who have helped me at various stages of this book. Without their encouragement, chivvying, and cheerful insistence that I get on with it, this book would have continued to languish on disk. Thanks to Susan Strehle, whose course on modern U.S. fiction helped hatch this project. Many thanks are due to my dissertation director, Bill Spanos, whose electrifying fusion of scholarly and political passions provided me with my first academic fix. I am also greatly endebted to John Tagg. Our exhausting discussions of cultural theory and the ways in which it might illuminate my study of immigrant women, together with his rigorous and astute critique of early drafts of the manuscript, helped improve this project immeasurably.

At George Mason University, I have been fortunate in finding a group of humane, empathetic, and highly professional colleagues. Thanks to Eileen Sypher and David Kaufmann for their comments on various chapters; to Devon Hodges for her incisive critique of the manuscript and also for her periodic reminders to me to "keep writing" despite the press of teaching and other professional duties; and to Deborah Kaplan, whose perceptive reading of the early chapters and general enthusiasm for the project provided a much-needed tonic at a critical juncture. Barbara Melosh has helped me in every conceivable way, and I am especially grateful to her. She has provided me with savvy readings of multiple drafts of each chapter, given sage advice in negotiating the academic minefield, and been a constant source of general support and encouragement. She has been a wonderful colleague and an exemplary department chair.

I'm grateful to my students at George Mason for their patience and willingness to engage with my somewhat obsessional interest in issues pertaining to race, immigration, and maternity: their creative and thoughtful exploration of these issues has been invigorating and highly gratifying. A special thanks to Jane Buckley, Felicia Carr, Craig Fordney, Darrin Johnson, Laura Matthews, Monica McTyre, Angela Nepodal, Noreen Sait, Janice Silverstein, and Susan Wilson.

Thanks are also due to my editor at the University of Illinois Press, Emily Rogers. Her efficiency and expeditious handling of the manuscript have made the process of bringing this book to press a relatively seamless and thoroughly pleasurable one. I would also like to thank the editors at *College Literature* and *Modern Fiction Studies,* where earlier versions of chapters 2 and 5 first appeared. Their permission to reprint is appreciated.

Finally, and most of all, I'd like to thank Desiree Beck. Her good humor, equability, and irrepressible optimism form a necessary context for my academic pursuits and—best of all—reduce such pursuits to their proper perspective.

Introduction:
"Amazing Racial Hybrids and Ethnic Horrors":
Race and the Immigrant Woman, 1890–1925

> When, at last, interest was directed upon [the immigrants'] . . . peculiar status
> in the cultural complex of American life. . . . Protecting the immigrant;
> restraining him; keeping him out; compelling him to conform to ourselves;
> doing at least something to the immigrant and especially talking all sorts of
> phantasies about him, became the order of the day.
>
> —Horace Kallen, "'Americanization'"

> In a field of discourse like racism what is generally circulated and exchanged is
> not simply truth but truth claims or representations. These representations
> draw their efficacy from traditions, conventions, institutions, and tacit modes
> of mutual comprehension.
>
> —David Theo Goldberg

IN 1993, *Time* magazine, riding a wave of anti-immigrant paranoia that has not yet crested, published a special issue entitled "The New Face of America." Using a software package ("Morph 2") borrowed from a special effects department in Hollywood, the magazine assembled, out of seven distinct "racial types," a composite image of the future national physiognomy.[1] Although the magazine admitted that the "extremely complex" nature of the "not yet fully understood" ("Rebirth" 66) rules of genetic engineering made such an enterprise, in terms of any scientific pretensions, impossible, the magazine instead employed a software gimmick ("used to produce . . . Michael Jackson's celebrated metamorphosis in his *Black or White* video") that tapped into and helped recycle the nation's most egregious—although not its most long-lived—form of nativism: racial paranoia.[2]

The last great wave of xenophobia had its inception in the early 1890s and centered on a "scientific" (eugenic) fear of "mongrelization" from the influx of immigrants from Southern and Eastern Europe. The institution of a racially motivated national origins quota system in 1924, which favored Northern European immigrants and remained intact until the 1960s, effectively quieted this nativist upheaval.[3] *Time* had reached back to this period for its rhetoric in order to bring subsequent immigration history up to date. Fears of "race suicide" resonated in the magazine's warning that "the U.S [has] undert[aken] a basic shift in national policy . . . [which] favor[s] . . . Third World nations. . . . the U.S. before long will have to redefine just who its minorities are" ("America's Challenge" 3).

The composite visage *Time* chose to place on its cover was that of a female. The editors paired it with a story about a mishap with the morph program that had produced a grotesque female figure: "a distinctively feminine face—sitting atop a muscular neck and hairy chest" ("Rebirth" 66). The juxtaposition of this tale of the generation of a genetic nightmare with the image of a comely cover girl recalls the turn-of-the-century rhetoric on immigration. Stephen Crane's *Maggie: A Girl of the Streets,* published exactly a century earlier (1893), provides similar twinned women: an Irish mother who has "immense hands" (8), "massive shoulders" (7), and a "great chest" (12) and her daughter, who is "a most rare and wonderful production of a tenement district, a pretty girl" (16). As in *Time* magazine, the figure of the attractive female immigrant augurs and embodies the serendipitously effective melting pot, but she is attended by her necessary inverse, a monstrous, manlike woman whose sexual indeterminacy portends the potentially disastrous results of America's racial experiments.

In both moments, the figure of the alien woman moves into the foreground as the immigrant debate acquires racialist contours. To a striking degree, representations of immigrant women dominated the last great nativist convulsion, covering roughly the years from 1890 to 1925. This book examines the prevalence, contexts, and uses of those representations. As Horace Kallen pointed out in 1924, the previous twenty years had witnessed a proliferation of discourses, or, as he put it, an intensification of the production of "phantasies" about the nature of the immigrant and "his" contribution to American life (129). And even the most cursory review of this literature reveals that it is the immigrant woman who is, for native writers, the generative source of these "phantasies."

All kinds of publications took up the issue of immigration during the 1890s and first two decades of the twentieth century: scholarly works in the emergent fields of anthropology and sociology as well as philosophy (Franz Boas, Randolph Bourne, Sophonisba Breckinridge, William Ripley, and E. A. Ross); economic tracts (Francis Walker and Richmond Mayo Smith); social workers' reports from the front (Lillian Wald and Elsa Herzfeld); personal reminiscences (Jane Addams); muckraking exposés (Jacob Riis and Upton Sinclair); and imaginative literature (Willa Cather, Stephen Crane, Harold Frederic, Fannie Hurst, and Frank Norris). Special-interest periodicals, such as the journal of social work, *The Survey,* and

Immigrants in America Review, lavished attention on the increasingly contentious issue of the "new" immigration and the particularly critical problem of immigrant women, while more longstanding and august periodicals (*Atlantic Monthly* and *Century Magazine*) as well as daily newspapers devoted more and more column space to consideration of the multiple facets of the controversy.

The set of representations found in these texts constituted and set the terms of a debate that raged until the mid-1920s about the future of immigration and the future makeup of the United States. And all writers, no matter what their ideological position—nativism ("scientific" racism), Americanization, or cultural pluralism—drew upon discourses that articulated feminine gender in order to construct an immigrant woman who would, in turn, embody their particular version of the immigrant "problem."[4] Drawing on the work of Edward Said, David Goldberg has pointed to the peculiarly parasitic nature of racist discourse: It taps into "traditions, conventions, institutions and tacit modes of mutual comprehension" (298), always based upon already constituted categories of meaning. In the case of the immigrant in turn-of-the-century America, such categories consisted of a series of current cultural narratives on the female gender.

For many Progressive Era writers, the figure of the immigrant mother proved particularly resonant. For nativists, who linked the alien woman's imputed preternatural fecundity with eugenically based theories concerning the effects of miscegenation, the maternal function of the immigrant woman was especially productive of racial anxiety. They warned of the "'chaotic constitution'" (Ross 289) being formed from the influx of immigrants, predicting imminent race suicide and race mongrelization. Madison Grant, for example, alerted native Americans to the "amazing racial hybrids and . . . ethnic horrors" being spawned in the neighborhoods of New York (92). Drawing on discourses concerning the sexually transgressive and "unruly" female body, nativists successfully inserted biological concerns into the debate about immigration restriction.[5] In turn, Americanizers and cultural pluralists tapped into various aspects of the discourse of sentimental motherhood in order to formulate their own positions. My concern in this book is to delineate how immigrant femininity, particularly immigrant maternity, became an entrenched site of representational struggle within the public discussion of immigration.

The contours of these representations of immigrant women were decisively inflected by—and constituted a complex response to—the critical economic and social shifts underway in the United States at the turn of the nineteenth century. The discursive production of immigration as a problem of national significance occurred simultaneously with the transformation of capitalism. The instantiation of Fordist capitalism and the manifold cultural ramifications of that economic restructuring were not merely backdrops to the story of the racialization of the immigrant woman. Rather, the particular representations of the immigrant woman that emerged constituted specific responses to, and negotiations of, distinct aspects of the ongoing transition. For example, the excoriation of the "biological parsimony" of the foreign woman, found frequently within the writings of nativist economists, was an attempt to construct a consensus about the wisdom of stricter immigration controls. At the same time, the constancy and frequency of this representation of the avaricious immigrant woman must also be seen as a negotiation of the ongoing transition from a production-based economy to one based on consumption. It reveals a native ambivalence about abandoning older ideals of thrift for newer injunctions to indulge and spend. Again, the cultural pluralists' construction of the immigrant woman as a primitive earth mother was an attempt to foment an antirestrictionist temper among the public. Simultaneously, their immigrant "primitive" articulated a particular, and largely negative, reaction to the speed and direction of modernization.

My analysis assumes the material character of discursive structures. As I examine the complex and contradictory set of depictions of immigrant women at the turn of the nineteenth century, I recognize that such representations had real social and economic effects on the lives of those so persistently and willfully spoken for. Immigration reform activists' depiction of culturally inept foreign mothers, for example, led to the implementation of a number of social programs designed to address that backwardness. These programs promoted direct intervention into immigrant women's daily lives in order to reform their child-rearing methods, culinary and domestic skills, and consumption habits.

At the same time, following Ernesto Laclau and Chantal Mouffe, I assume that terms such as *race* and *immigrant woman* are "floating signifiers" and that the process of anchoring those signifiers within particular complexes of meaning occurs through representational struggle. Thus, any particular definition of immigrant women had to contend with a number of other divergent definitions as nativists, Americanizers, and cultural pluralists all attempted to endow the signifier *immigrant woman* with particular and distinctly different kinds of resonance. Therefore, a definitive "fixing" of that signifier was ultimately impossible. I assume, however, that the relative cultural currencies of, for example, the nativist version of the immigrant woman as a mindlessly reproducing throwback or the cultural pluralist construction of the immigrant woman as primitive earth mother had key effects on the nature of the immigration legislation eventually implemented.[6] The institution of a national origins quota system in 1924 (the Johnson-Reed Act) makes it possible to surmise that the version of immigrant woman articulated by nativists ultimately proved most persuasive to legislators and public opinion in general.

I have discussed the key use of the figure of the immigrant woman in helping to racialize the European immigrant and her circulation within distinctly different discourses of race. Drawing on the work of Paul Gilroy, I track the articulation of various kinds of racism at the site of the representation of the immigrant female. Gilroy observes that "racial meanings can change, can be struggled over" and adds, "Rather than talking about racism in the singular, analysts should therefore be talking about racisms in the plural. These are not just different over time but may vary within the same social formation or historical conjuncture" (38).[7]

The immigration controversy constituted a particularly intense moment of struggle around race, and I will examine three racializing discourses that circulated at the turn of the nineteenth century: nativism, which drew on elaborate "scientific" theories to buttress its account of biologically based racial difference; Americanization, which explained race as a function of environment and culture; and cultural pluralism, which oscillated between viewing race as a product of culture and as a product of biology but in either case argued that the qualities of alien races were precisely what American culture needed and should welcome. Each form drew upon narratives of femininity and maternity already circulating within the culture to articulate a particular version of the "immigrant problem."

I draw extensively on the fiction of the period and provide detailed readings of Willa Cather's *My Ántonia* (1918), Stephen Crane's *Maggie* (1893), Harold Frederic's *The Damnation of Theron Ware* (1896), and Frank Norris's *McTeague* (1899). Jacob Riis's *How the Other Half Lives* (1890) provides the focal point of analysis within a further chapter. An important example of early documentary photography, Riis's work has also been read for its aesthetic and synthetic qualities, and it is from that perspective that I approach his work. Critics have begun to read these narratives within the context of the "racial-ethnic" concerns of the period.[8] The centrality of the immigrant mother therein has gone largely unremarked, however. This book examines the maternal representations found in these fictions against the context of that larger restrictionist discourse that began to permeate the culture during the 1890s, a discourse in which the immigrant mother also played a key role.

Each chapter proceeds by limning the distinctive construction of the immigrant woman found within the academic and periodical literature produced by the advocates of a particular immigration policy. My aim in tracking these analyses of the specific challenges (in the case of the nativists and Americanizers) and benefits (in the pluralist case) posed to the nation by the influx of foreign women is twofold. First, I establish that each of these partisan groups imagined a peculiar kind of immigrant woman and trace the political and scientific substrate of that specific representation. Second, by contacting a substantial number, as well as a significant variety, of such nonfiction sources, my analysis also suggests the degree of regularity of the narrative's occurrence.

I then examine a fictional text in which a particular construction of the alien female is both reproduced and further crystalized. For example, I describe the narrative anxiety attending the spectacle of the overly fecund immigrant woman in Stephen Crane's *Maggie* against the larger eugenic discourse systematically laid out in the work of nativist writers such as E. A. Ross and Madison Grant; I consider Norris's character Trina in *McTeague* in the context of the "racial economic" discourse of nativist economists; I argue that Riis's representations of immigrant maternity clearly draw from and contribute to the discourse of Americanization; and, finally, I contend that Willa Cather's depiction of her eponymous heroine, Ántonia, clearly derives from and helps constitute the larger discourse of cultural pluralism. Although each chapter moves from a discussion of nonfiction to an analysis of the fictional variants of a particular racialist narrative, I do not mean to suggest the direction of influence of these ideas and concerns. Rather, discrete racialist narratives emerged unevenly across the discursive field, surfacing simultaneously, albeit haltingly, across many different kinds of genres.

The fictional incarnations of immigrant women are especially useful because they illustrate the ubiquity of these representations within the culture as a whole rather than solely within the texts of those activists and thinkers consciously agitated by and explicitly concerned with the issue of immigrant restriction. For example, the fact that the nativist perception of the immigrant woman as the active agent of racial degeneration informs *Maggie* as well as *McTeague* illustrates that this eugenic narrative had, by the turn of the century, acquired substantial cultural currency. Thus, I am emphatically not concerned to argue that Stephen Crane was avowedly nativist (in fact, the evidence suggests that he was not) or that Harold Frederic was incipiently so.[9] Indeed, that Crane's expressed views appear devoid of explicit nativist sentiment further confirms, in the context of *Maggie*'s eugenic subtext, the hegemonic status of the nativist narrative within the culture at large.

My approach to the fictional representations of the racialized immigrant woman is guided by the assumption that imaginative literature is not simply infused with ideology but itself performs "cultural work."[10] These novels' recounting of particular narratives about the implications of the alien influx helped in their dissemination, especially because the audience for the novels extended beyond, or at least was not necessarily coterminous with, those readers drawn to the rather arid economic tracts of Francis Amasa Walker or to the philosophical ruminations of Horace Kallen. In addition, fictional narratives possess a distinct ideological valency. As Frederic Jameson reminds us, the popularity of the form derives from its capacity to "invent . . . imaginary or formal 'solutions'" to contemporaneous social problems (79). Accordingly, the following pages also limn the discrete imaginative solutions these novels pose to the ever more perplexing presence of the alien female.

Although these fictions help establish the pervasiveness of racializing narratives in discussions of the immigration issue at the end of the century, I do not mean to suggest that their depictions were never resisted or otherwise negotiated. Meanings are never transmitted seamlessly from text to reader, and certainly "there is frequent tension between the received interpretation and practical experience" (Williams 130). However, this book is not principally concerned with ascertaining the degree to which the general populace accepted and subscribed to these racializing narratives.[11] Although my analysis may indirectly cast light on that issue, my focus is on these narratives' discursive instantiation and circulation. Accordingly, I track the relatively formal and well-articulated systems of meanings produced around the figure of the immigrant woman in both nonfictional and imaginative texts.

In my efforts to trace recurrent patterns of representations of the immigrant woman, I have focused on their continuities within particular texts and across selected groups of texts. All texts are ruptured, contradictory, and—to a greater or lesser degree—ideologically heteropathic. Too, Michel Foucault's definition of discourse as constitutively discontinuous and fragmented renders chimerical the attempt to read a particular discursive position as seamlessly embodied in a specific text. Nativist rhetoric leaks, at particular points, into both Riis's *How the Other Half Lives* and Cather's *My Ántonia,* and an environmentally based racialism surfaces, at moments, in Crane's *Maggie.* In the interests of defining particular images of the immigrant woman within a specific sociocultural moment, as well as of tracking the cultural work they perform, I will trace the boldest contours of each text's representation of that figure.[12]

Chapter 1 sets the context for the emergence of the immigrant woman at the center of the reanimated controversy over immigration. Historians have agreed that during the last decade of the nineteenth century an elaborate classificatory schema was set in place that distinguished between the racial traits of the new and the old immigration.[13] William Z. Ripley's *The Races of Europe* (1899) was a central text in the elaboration of the category of the new immigrant. I discuss this work in tandem with the writings of Gustave Michaud and Harold Frederic and demonstrate that, collectively, these texts construct the racial traits of the new immigration on the basis of normative gender templates. Each narrative represented the new immigration as a definitively feminized group; however, the writers were not necessarily nativist. They all argued that the feminine qualities of new immigrants rendered them a particularly valuable addition to the national race pool. Despite that view, their feminization of the new immigrant ultimately set the discursive stage for a full-blown nativist argument. Taking up and elaborating Ripley's and Michaud's racial classifications in a pejorative direction, Madison Grant and Henry Pratt Fairchild would call for the cessation of immigration in order to protect native Anglo-Saxon vigor from this feminized incursion. Within their restrictionist arguments, the immigrant woman, the "ur-female" of an already feminized race, emerged as the central locus of concern.

In the second chapter I deal with this eugenically based discourse and examine the nativists' construction of the immigrant woman as a reproductive threat to national integrity. In a series of articles appearing in journals such as *Century Magazine, North American Review,* and *Forum,* writers such Robert DeCourcy Ward, Edward Alsworth Ross, Francis Walker, Madison Grant, and Henry Cabot Lodge underscored the racial inferiority and unassimilability of the new immigrant. That discursive strategy was, as John Higham has indicated, part of a concerted attempt to influence immigrant legislation. Robert DeCourcy Ward helped in 1894 to form the Immigration Restriction League, a group in which Cabot Lodge was particularly active and whose early efforts were focused on instituting a literacy test as a condition of admittance for all immigrants (Higham, *Strangers* 102–5). Subscribing to a biologistic racism, nativists believed that the Anglo-Saxon race represented the true American stock and that immigrants constituted "beaten men from beaten races" (Walker, "Restriction" 828). Their inherent inferiority was contained in their blood or "germ-plasm" and transmitted to future generations. Specifically, this degeneration was contained within the female of the species. Repeatedly, nativists pinpointed alien women rather than men as principle carriers of degenerate genes. I will examine how two specific discourses, one concerning biological race and one centering on the figure of the "unruly, grotesque" woman but both dealing with issues of location and containment, were articulated together in nativist texts to produce the immigrant woman as a racial and sexual threat to the Republic. Chapter 2 also contains an extended analysis of Stephen Crane's *Maggie: A Girl of the Streets.* Insofar as it presents the mindlessly proliferating alien female as the preeminent symbol and agent of the racial disaster portended by immigration, the novel reveals its debt to the eugenic narrative, which, in turn, it helped crystalize.

Chapter 3 pursues the nativists' construction of the immigrant woman while shifting attention to her centrality within their economic arguments. Nativists did not confine their warnings about the deleterious effects of immigration to a discussion of stock contamination. Some of the earliest proto-nativist thinkers, such as Richmond Mayo-Smith and Francis A. Walker, were economists. Against the claims of businessmen that cheap immigrant labor was necessary to the nation's financial health, they argued that immigrants were detrimental to fiscal well-being. Nativist economists forged a racial-economic argument that held that immigrants' innate parsimony and preference for slovenly living conditions rendered them constitutionally unfitted for a consumer economy. And it was immigrant women, in whom the role of spending for the family was vested, who were depicted as the chief culprits in this perverse and destructive underconsumption. Representing the immigrant woman as biologically averse to spending, nativist economists argued that her atavistic mania for accumulation placed her at odds with the needs of an emergent consumer economy. Frank Norris's *McTeague* (1899) provides an exemplary instance of this economic rhetoric.

But it was not merely nativists who discovered the problem of immigration. In chapter 4, I cull widely from the texts produced by those social workers, settlement house residents, and sociologists whose concept of racial reformation and particular reform agendas mark them as Americanizers (Elsa Herzfeld, Lillian Wald, Katherine Anthony, and Jacob Riis); from the works of government representatives affiliated with the official Americanization movement (Frances Kellor and Kate Waller Barrett); and from academics commissioned to produce studies of particular aspects of Americanization (Sophonisba Breckinridge and Peter Speek). As cultural rather than biological racists, these Americans were concerned to have aliens rid themselves of their Old World culture as expeditiously as possible. They believed that immigrants were capable of being improved, and the task they set themselves was precisely that. Their texts positioned immigrant women within a familiar and normalizing discourse: sentimental motherhood. Paradoxically, although this construction was intended to demonstrate her potential for normative citizenship it also reified her as constitutionally assimilable. Nativists located the intransigence of the immigrant woman's difference within a racialized genetic schema. By contrast, it was the Americanizers' investment in genetically based explanations of gender difference that convinced them of her implacable racial stasis.

The cultural pluralists' version of the immigrant woman began to circulate in the early teens. Horace Kallen, Randolph Bourne, Jane Addams, Edith Abbott, and the novelists Willa Cather and Fannie Hurst were the most prominent pluralists. In chapter 5, I consider their deployment of the image of the immigrant woman. As disaffected moderns who increasingly perceived themselves to be out of place in a rapidly commodifying and homogeneous society, they constructed the immigrant as a primitive other poised to save U.S. culture from its meretricious tendencies. Despite their antimodern stance, the pluralists' obsessive recycling of the immigrant woman's primitive maternalism abetted the economic needs of a burgeoning U.S. economy. My reading of Willa Cather's *My Ántonia* establishes that pluralist discourse, no less than nativism, helped normalize the racial stratification of the labor market and encouraged the exploitation of immigrant women's labor in particular.

Before moving to these specific analyses, I will address two related issues. First is the question of why, when the immigrant "problem" began to be formulated almost entirely in terms of race, recourse to the immigrant woman, especially the immigrant mother, became persistent. The second issue concerns how the racialization of the European immigrant abutted the ongoing discursive construction of that other, definitively racialized, category in postbellum U.S. culture, the African-American woman.

The preeminence of the immigrant woman, especially the immigrant mother, is all the more striking given that substantially fewer women immigrated to the United States during this period than men. The Dillingham Commission reported that "from 1869 to 1910 the percentage of males [among immigrants] was 64.9. Of every 1000 immigrants in 1910, 707 were males, and 293 females" (United States Immigration Commission 59).[14] How to account for this rhetorical stress on alien maternity, despite the immigrant woman's disproportion in real terms? One might begin by pointing out that the iconography of maternity, as a site at which particular conceptions of nationhood can be articulated and contested, has been a particularly powerful resource in various cultures and diverse historical moments.[15]

Within the U.S. context, historians have pointed to the elaboration of the discourse of private and public space in the nineteenth century and to the concomitant mapping of that division as a gendered one.[16] This discourse constructed the domesticated, native, white woman's body, in its relationship to the home, as mainspring and guarantor of the nation's health. The "Cult of True Womanhood," which confirmed and mandated woman's inevitable destiny as mother, worked to contain female sexuality. It contributed to the "hysterization of women's bodies" (Foucault, *History of Sexuality* 104) that marked the female body off as "saturated with sexuality" and positioned it, as Foucault points out, "In organic communication with the social body (whose regulated fecundity it was supposed to ensure), the family space (of which it had to be a substantial and functional element), and the life of children (which it produced and had to guarantee, by virtue of a biologico-moral responsibility)" (104). Within that discourse, continued political order depended on preserving the safe space of woman's sphere, the home, which was metonymically related to the inviolate body of the woman.[17] By an extension of this logic, the body of the white, middle-class woman, corralled within the space of the home, assumed a metaphoric relation to the larger body of the Republic.[18]

Her ability to so signify was premised on the abjection of other groups of women—African American or working class, for example—whose maternity figured as monstrous and nationally cataclysmic. Eva Cherniavsky explains that "*Both* the commodified (black) *and* the naturalized (white) reproductive bodies become . . . legible . . . in opposition to each other (i.e., mothers are not black; black women are not mothers)" (xi). Yet even with regard to white, middle-class women, the equation of maternity with national integrity was not, by any means, unproblematic. Stephanie Smith has shown that recourse to a (monstrous) image of maternity in order to connote national upheaval and dis-ease was at least as prevalent during the nineteenth century as was the use of that figure to invoke republican integrity (14–16).[19] Representations of the maternal that signified "utopian perfection" (3) were, even with regard to the normative, white, middle-class mother, consistently disrupted by images of the maternal as "unpredictable, perhaps ungovernable" (60). In short, the elaboration of the ideal of True Womanhood, with all its constitutive variants, deviations, and antitheses, was a particularly labile lexicon during the nineteenth and twentieth centuries and was used and retooled to articulate a variety of positions within particular political debates.

That rather generalized explanation does not allow consideration of what, in the specific racial and gender discourses of late-nineteenth- and early-twentieth-century America, might have facilitated their mutual articulation. It seems clear that the prominence of the science of eugenics within nativist thinking threw the figure of the immigrant mother into relief for those writers. As Laura Doyle has argued, eugenic thinking "entangled any public discussion of motherhood and sexuality in the questions of race and nation" (20).[20] This eugenic reasoning provides a partial account of why the question of race and the female sex become mutually constitutive at this historical juncture. It cannot, however, adequately address the reason why even the racializing discourses that explicitly denied biology as a factor in racial formation returned obsessively to the key figure of the immigrant woman—especially the immigrant mother. Part of the ease with which they became linked is attributable to the centrality of the concept of the family, at that particular historical juncture, to the discursive elaboration of both woman and race. The idea of the family is key to a number of racist discourses and, equally, key to the construction of woman within turn-of-the-century America.[21] The immigrant woman, particularly the mother, positioned at the conjuncture of both formations, emerges as central to the elaboration of race in the period.

Kwame Anthony Appiah has pointed out that "the metaphor of family is often invoked by racism" (14). In many racist tracts there is an "assimilation of 'race feeling' to 'family feeling.'" This issues in "intrinsic racism" (10), a theoretical justification for prejudice on the grounds that, as with one's family, it is natural to prefer people of one's own race. Similarly, Martin Barker argues that the "new" racism that emerged in Britain during the 1970s and the 1980s was based on tribalism, the idea that "it is only natural to meet strangers with hostility" (76). Barker quotes sociobiologist Edward Wilson as a key exemplar of this view: "'Nationalism and racism, to take two examples, are the culturally nurtured outgrowths of simple tribalism'" (98). For these sociobiologists, "'Simple tribalism' (what-

ever that may be) is just kin altruism in action. It is simply the extension of loving one's family" (98). Within late-nineteenth-century America, the analogy
between family and race was an equally naturalized one. Indeed, Priscilla Wald
argues that the Americanization effort was intended to ameliorate "the crisis
facing the *literal* 'American' (traditional white middle-class) family" (246). That
crisis, in turn, was seen to "threaten . . . the nation, the metaphoric 'American
family,' with potential extinction, with becoming 'nothing at all'" (246).[22]

The centrality of the concept of the family to that of race takes more concrete
forms within specific racial discourses. Racist discourse, whether biologically or
culturally grounded, views the racially distinct family unit as a site in which the
reproduction of difference is accomplished.[23] To the racism that holds that an
inferior gene pool or blood is passed on from one generation to the next, the
family, as the site of physical reproduction (with the woman as the main organ
of that reproduction), is seen as the place where racially inferior individuals are
propagated. It therefore becomes a particular target for racist opprobrium.
Within late-nineteenth-century America, for example, nativist anxiety over immigration produced the fear of race suicide—the idea that inferior races were
breeding at a faster rate than native Americans and that failure to act would be
suicide on the part of true Americans.[24] Tenements, seen as places where immigrant families gathered to breed, were therefore demonized in the writings of
nativists. The immigrant mother, through whom the race was perpetuated, took
on critical importance. As Madison Grant formulated the issue, "No ethnic conquest can be complete unless . . . the invaders bring their own women with them.
If the conquerors [i.e., recent immigrants] are obliged to depend on the women
of the vanquished to carry on the race, the intrusive blood strain in a short time
becomes diluted beyond recognition" (71). The immigrant family, sequestered
within the space of the tenement, thus became the target of nativist hatred, and
the immigrant mother, spawning a myriad of racial throwbacks, embodied the
racial threat in a particularly concrete way.

Even for those who believed that racial difference was a matter of cultural or
environmental difference, the family emerged as critical to the definition of race.
Paul Gilroy has pointed out that, for a specific type of contemporary British racist,
"'Race' differences are displayed in culture which is reproduced in educational
institutions and, above all, in family life" (43). In the same cultural context, Errol
Lawrence has analyzed the way "black cultures and more specifically black house-
holds have been constructed as 'problem categories' posing difficulties for themselves and for society at large" ("Just Plain Common Sense" 74). The nuclear
family is presented as the critical site for the inculcation of civilization and the
black family as dysfunctional and incapable of such inculcation.

Gilroy's and Lawrence's arguments concerning the centrality of family in the racialization of Britain's black diasporic populations have counterparts in work that discusses the racialization of African Americans. The work of the Park school of sociology in the 1920s and 1930s focused on the supposed breakdown of the black family and explained its "pathology" as a legacy of slavery. Within late-nineteenth-century America, too, a similar type of "cultural racism" saw the immigrant home as "the place where 'primary socialization' takes place and where 'culture' is reproduced" (Lawrence, "Just Plain Common Sense" 50). The immigrant home was constructed as dysfunctional in this respect, and Americanizers repeatedly argued the need for native intervention within that space.

Simultaneously, within the late nineteenth and early twentieth centuries the family was seen as the woman's sphere. Even those women who fell outside the parameters of the home, who refused wifehood or motherhood, or who could not afford to devote their time solely to the domestic realm (prostitutes and working women, for example) were all defined in relation to what they were not: home-makers and full-time mothers. Hence, within the Americanizer's discourse, two notions—one concerning the family as the sphere of woman's influence and the other concerning the family as central to the inculcation of the requisite culture and hence as the key to assimilation—came together to underscore the importance of the immigrant woman within the racialist schema. For Americanizers, then, it was particularly imperative to reach the immigrant mother, poised as she was to inculcate either New or Old World ways in her children. Cultural pluralists did not deny that racial difference inhered in a culture transmitted by mother to offspring, but they argued for the value of these differences. It was, perhaps, equally apposite that the immigrant mother should figure centrally in their texts as the critical conduit and preserver of valuable traditions and mores fast disappearing from a rapidly modernizing and commodified culture.

The primary role of the immigrant mother across a variety of racisms recalls the prominent figure of the black woman in the racialization of African Americans and raises the question of the relationship between the two constructions. It has been amply documented that the turn of the nineteenth century produced increasingly intensive racialization of African Americans in the wake of Reconstruction. Patricia Morton, summarizing previous scholarship, has pointed out that although the African-American male was constructed as a sexual menace threatening societal order, within the fields of historiography and sociology the African American woman, too, was given a central position within the melodramatic schema of race conflict. She cites influential historian Phillip Alexander Bruce's *The Plantation Negro as a Freeman* (1889) as a representative depiction of a depraved black mother responsible for her family's pathology. The supposed sexual avidity of the black woman, freed from slavery's "civilizing" influence, wrought havoc upon her family (28). And it was this licentiousness that turned the black man toward the rape of white women, looking there for the qualities he could not find among his own women (28). As a biological racist, Bruce attributed this putative sexual appetite to innate depravity. Sociologists of the Park school at the University of Chicago, thirty years later, would proffer environmental and cultural reasons for such licentiousness while still pinpointing this supposed maternal moral turpitude as key to the black family's problems (Morton, *Disfigured Images* 70–71).

Thus, normative notions of middle-class femininity and morality converge with the race-family equation to construct both the immigrant and the African-American woman as deleterious to the health of the nation. Yet what becomes clear from a comparative analysis of the representations of both groups is the degree to which each racialization was distinctly inflected by both the history and tradition of representation of each group and by the cultural work each specific racist discourse performed. Simply put, although the racialization of African Americans and immigrants both draw on a common body of work in eugenics, on a set of theories concerning the depredations of environment on the family, and on the central function of the woman within the family, the racialized immigrant mother and the racialized black mother are sharply differentiated.

To illustrate, I will sketch the kinds of cultural work that the representation of the racialized black woman has facilitated. Christine Stansell, drawing on a wealth of scholarship, observes that images of "parasitical black mothers" and "lascivious black teenage girls" are regularly evoked within contemporary debates on welfare and abortion funding ("White Feminists" 262).[25] Such figures are part of a particularly resilient twinned construction of black women that can be traced to the antebellum South, that of the Mammy/Jezebel figures: "Aunt Jemima has an opposite, Jezebel, as sexy as the mammy is sexless . . . not mother but prostitute" (Roberts, *Myth of Aunt Jemima* 2). These twinned stereotypes served particular functions within the economy of slavery. Whereas the Mammy figure projected a myth of nurturing black femininity that fostered the idea that slavery "promoted racial affection, but not, as Northern abolitionists charged, illicit sexual intimacy," the Jezebel justified sexual and physical exploitation by presenting black women as innately lascivious and "as a sexual animal—not a real woman at all" (Morton, *Disfigured Images* 10).[26] Of course, the Mammy/Jezebel couplet faced off against the Southern Lady, all three phantasms reinforcing "the white man's sexual control over all women" (9).[27]

The stereotype has been retooled in every generation according to the needs of the particular sociocultural moment. Thus, the figure of the Mammy was heavily circulated after Reconstruction as "a major symbol of the idealization of Jim Crow segregation" (Morton, *Disfigured Images* 35). Her submissiveness toward whites was matched only by her aggressiveness toward blacks, especially black males (Jewell, *From Mammy to Miss America* 38). Jumping forward roughly fifty years, in the Moynihan Report the supposed independence and strength of the Mammy figure, as well as her nurturance of the white family, became transmuted into an excessive independence and agency that traumatized the male and caused his desertion and the break up of the family.[28] Too, the sexuality of the Jezebel figure had become part of Moynihan's black mother, another instance of her damaging independence. As Toni Morrison put it in a collection of essays dealing with the inextricable links between the reception of Anita Hill's testimony during the Hill-Thomas hearings and time-worn racial stereotypes, such representations are "interchangeable fictions from a utilitarian menu and can be mixed and matched to suit any racial palette" (*Race-ing Justice* xv)—or, one might add, particular sociopolitical need.

Looking at the racialized immigrant woman, we find no corresponding Mammy figure. Although within the literature of cultural pluralism the immigrant mother becomes an image of fecund nature posited as an antidote to the depredations of a commodity culture, the image of the nurturing immigrant mother found in these texts is significantly different to that of the Mammy. Willa Cather's character, Ántonia, although a nurturing, maternal figure, is no Mammy. By text's end, she nurtures her own family, not that of her white neighbors. She is retiring and diffident rather than aggressive, and Cather seems anxious to make an overt distinction between them through the use of physical characteristics. Ántonia is significantly described as "flat chested and toothless," the very antithesis of the stereotypical Aunt Jemima.[29]

The disparate histories of the immigrant and African American populations in their relation to dominant white culture account for this distinctive difference. The Mammy figure emerged out of the convergence of specific historical realities, particularly the black woman's history of nanny service to whites, as well as the psychological need to create a figure who would allay scruples about the ethics of slavery—and later segregation.[30] Lacking such a history, and enshrouded always within an extremely prevalent sociological analysis that stressed the difficulties many immigrant women in particular had in adapting to American culture, the nurturing immigrant mother emerges as diffident within her family and unacquainted, or uncomfortable with, the broader social arena.

This sociological truism might also be said to play into the differential constructions of the ineffective immigrant, as opposed to the domineering black, mother. As I argue in chapter 4, writers as various as Jacob Riis and Lillian Wald pinpointed the immigrant mother both as central to the effective assimilation of her children and as lacking in that realm. At first glance, such constructions appear similar to the ongoing construction of the black mother as the key to the pathology of the black family. The failings attributed to both were very different, however, and sprang from specific histories and traditions of representations. For genetic racists, the break up of black families was directly traceable to the innate licentiousness of black women. Within the work of the Park school of sociology, that licentiousness was not contested but interpreted as a legacy of slavery (Morton, *Disfigured Images* 75). Similarly. the black woman's work outside the home "was said to make her uncontrollable by . . . [her husband] and hence, sexually independent and . . . dominant" (74).

Such descriptions contrast markedly with the social workers' and sociologists' construction of the reasons for the demise of the immigrant family home. If a black mother was excessively independent, both sexually and otherwise, an immigrant mother was constructed as excessively dependent. Her ignorance of American culture was repeatedly contrasted with the more rapid assimilation of her children and husband, whose participation in the worlds of labor and education facilitated that process. As Katherine Anthony described the limitations of such women, "The father has glimpses of the world, even if only from the driving seat of his truck. The son or daughter may go to work downtown . . . has thus a daily glimpse of something beyond the West Side. It is the mother of the family who least often sees beyond neighborhood limits" (6–7). Her backwardness with regard to New World ways led her children, it was surmised, to respect her insufficiently. Intervention into the home to alter that dependence was deemed crucial, because "too rapid Americanization of these children into pert young people without respect for authority is a dangerous problem" (Committee on Foreign-Born Women 213). The break up of immigrant family discipline and the much-discussed criminal tendency of the second generation were the results.

It is, perhaps, the figure of the Jezebel that resonates most closely with the representation of the immigrant woman in one of her variants. The Jezebel is an icon of lascivious black female sexuality drawn in opposition, at all points, to the figure of the pure white woman (Roberts, *Myth of Aunt Jemima* 4–5). In the slave economy, the image justified the master's sexual abuse; during the postbellum years the Jezebel figure as sexual predator was retooled under the aegis of eugenic theory and came to portend the racial degeneration that racial mixing would yield.[31] This insistence on the sexual ravenousness and moral depravity of the black woman is similar to a particular construction of the immigrant woman within nativist texts. Descriptions of the ruin of white men by sexually rapacious black women whose " 'uninhibited passions' and free offering of 'bodily favors' corrupted the white man, promoting his preference for 'the fellowship of dusky women' " (in Morton, *Disfigured Images* 31) are clearly replicated, for example in Frank Norris's story "A Case for Lombroso."

Yet, although mounting a similar critique of the racialized immigrant woman's sexual avidity, I would argue that Norris's depiction, even within nativist discourse, is atypical. A more prevalent depiction is that found in *Maggie*. Although the text draws on the same eugenicist rhetoric of racial degeneration in order to construct the sexualized immigrant woman as a threat to the health of the body politic, Stephen Crane is extremely hesitant to attribute a willful and active exercise of sexuality to her. The rapacious appetites and aggressive demeanor of the independently, and hence monstrously, sexual woman are projected onto Maggie's mother, however the immigrant prostitute herself emerges as a pathetic figure rather than an intentionally vicious one. Similarly, in E. A. Ross's *The Old World in the New*, the immigrant mother is depicted as a hapless tool of her mate in the latter's procession of race warfare: "It is the mothers who have to face anguish, exhaustion, and even death in the campaign to possess the land. Spending their women brutally, the Slavs advance; pitying their women, the Americans retreat" (134). In this phallic scenario, the images of the violently orgasmic foreign male (and the alien woman as the seed of the male) displace and recontain her aggressive fecundity while still positioning it as key to racial victory. Similarly, nativist texts as a whole refuse to ascribe an unmitigated predatory rapaciousness to immigrant women, although they are a threat to the extent that they are a repository of alien genes and portend interracial mixing.

Despite their common location at the convergence of race and family, the immigrant woman and the immigrant mother are significantly different from the female figures found within the dominant culture's representations of the black woman and mother during the period. What is most salient across the gamut of images of both groups is the differential ascription of agency to each. The sexually licentious black woman, the Mammy, and the overly independent black mother all possess a great deal of power and autonomy, although manifested in different forms and exercised in different realms. Across the spectrum of depictions of the racialized immigrant woman, however, her haplessness is repeatedly underscored.[32] Crane's inept prostitute, Riis's pathetic immigrant mother, and Jane Addams's distaff-clutching Italian peasant woman are singularly powerless figures. This state of being "passive and available for service" is, suggests Lauren Berlant, a constitutive element of what she dubs "the female body of the American National Symbolic," that iconic figure given material form in the Statue of Liberty and interpellating individuals as national subjects (27–28).[33]

Ironically, we could read the passivity and legibility of these immigrant women as testament to the degree to which they have already been naturalized. Harnessed to the task of defining the representative American state, whether through antithesis (nativism) or ideal incarnation (cultural pluralism), they take their place as normative female citizens through participating in the process of national self-definition. More particularly, however, the alien woman's imputed passivity suggests the larger political agenda to which those representations were yoked. The immigrant issue, a problem rediscovered relatively recently, was also one that appeared to be susceptible to native control. For those who saw immigration as portending a racial or cultural disaster, either legislation to cut off that flow or implementing Americanization programs seemed wholly viable means of controlling the problem. The figure of the passive immigrant woman was a fit adjunct to a debate that asserted a national ability to regulate at least this one aspect of the racial "problem," could the collective will to do so be mobilized.

1

A Rediscovered Problem:
Engendering the New Immigrant

> Foreigners are not coming to the United States in answer to any
> appetite of ours. . . . The lion . . . is having the food thrust down
> his throat, and his only alternative is, digest or die.
>
> —Josiah Strong, *Our Country*

> Our blood will in part be other than English blood. . . . the American
> population is henceforth to contain a smaller proportion of
> the energetic Baltic blood and a larger proportion of the art- and
> leisure-loving Mediterranean blood.
>
> —Franklin Giddings

REPRESENTATIONS OF immigrant women were produced, and must be understood, within the context of a general feminization of the alien influx that was accomplished in the final decade of the nineteenth century, when older forms of anti-immigrant feeling shifted to an explicit racialization of the alien along the axis of gender. William Z. Ripley provided the most systematic and influential elaboration in his magisterial *The Races of Europe,* which appeared in 1899. Spin-offs from that work continued to appear for a full decade, appearing in such weighty forums as the *Atlantic Monthly.*

Ripley's feminization of the alien was directly taken up in the work of sociologists and journalists such as Franklin Giddings and Gustave Michaud, respectively. Imaginative literature, too, recycled and contributed to the new form of anti-alien sentiment. Harold Frederic's novel *The Damnation of Theron Ware* (1896) clearly evinces the emergent animus. The text's treatment of an affluent Irish immigrant community (particularly its representation of Celia Madden, the community's chief luminary) reflects and helps solidify an ongoing gendering of the immigrant influx within the larger cultural context.

Ripley, Michaud, and Frederic ascribed distinct characteristics to particular immigrant groups and saw those traits as rooted, variously, in blood or culture.[1]

They were not, however, necessarily nativist. Rather, the group subscribed to that variant of the melting pot theory known as Anglo-American assimilationism.[2] Anglo-American assimilationists welcomed the racial traits of the alien as a subordinate component of a national racial makeup that would remain predominantly Anglo-Saxon. All three viewed the feminine qualities of new immigrants as a particularly valuable addition to the national race pool. Yet their feminization of the new immigrant ultimately set the discursive stage for a full-blown nativist argument. Recycling Ripley's racial classifications, Madison Grant, Henry Pratt Fairchild, and Edward Alsworth Ross, among others, would call for curtailing immigration in order to protect the native vigor of Anglo-Saxons from contamination by weak, effeminate aliens.

The feminization of the new immigrant was directly linked to the seismic socioeconomic shifts underway in the United States during the same period. Economic historian Martin Sklar identifies 1890 to 1916 as the major two and a half decades in which the economy was retooled from a "proprietary-competitive stage" to a "corporate-administered" phase.[3] David Harvey pinpoints 1914—when the $5, eight-hour day was introduced at Ford's Dearborn plant a year after the adoption of the assembly-line process—as the year the culture shifted toward what he, following Gramscian terminology, dubs the "Fordist" moment of capitalism (125). The manifold ramifications of that economic transition were played out at every level of the culture. Just as the various constructions of immigrant women were decisively inflected by particular aspects of this transition, so, too, the feminization of the new immigrant should be read within the context of specific cultural anxieties produced by the economic shift.

John Higham has elaborated the crucial role that William Ripley's *The Races of Europe* played in the "discovery" and racialization of the category of the new immigration.[4] Equally significant, however, is the role that Ripley's feminization of the non-Teutonic European played in that racialization. Ripley identified three European "sub-races": Teutons or Baltics from Northern Europe; Alpines, who were roughly Central European; and Mediterraneans, who hailed from Southern Europe. The latter two groups constituted the main source of the new immigration. Ripley described Teutons as "stolid, reserved, and independent" (208), whereas Alpines were depicted as strongly attached to home life and "inconstant, perhaps and fickle, nevertheless are quickly pacified after a passionate outbreak" (519). The representative Mediterranean, too, manifested "an innate impulsiveness" (536).

What is conspicuous about Ripley's classification is not only that the latter two groups collapse into one in opposition to the Teutonic but also that racial traits are elaborated on the basis of familiar nineteenth-century gender roles. The Alpine and the Mediterranean, like the idealized nineteenth-century woman, are represented as innately domestic and conservative as opposed to virile Anglo-Saxons, whose energetic enterprise facilitated the conquest of the Western world. Unlike those nativists who would take up his racialist schema, however, Ripley valued feminized traits as a positive addition to the national race composition.

Ripley's feminization of the immigrant rapidly gained cultural currency. Three years after the publication of his text, Gustave Michaud took up his classificatory schema and embellished it. Michaud's "What Shall We Be? The Coming Race in America" (1903) was published in *Century Magazine* and began by informing readers that the essay would address the question of the future race of the American people rather than the question of nationality. Whereas nationality is a function of environment and composed of the composite of "habits acquired by [the citizen] . . . through the institutions and agencies which surrounded him" (683), race is biologically based and intractable. Recapitulating and extending Ripley's descriptions of the traits of each European sub-race, Michaud wrote that Baltics (a term he preferred over, and used as a synonym for, Ripley's "Teutonic") "dedicate most of their time to work. . . . are liberally gifted with . . . moral instincts . . . [are] altruistic, fearless, honest and sincere. They love order and cleanliness" (686). By contrast, "the Alpine race is more given to meditation than to action. . . . They are endowed with powerful family affections" (686). Mediterraneans were described as "the most emotional of the three. . . . equally prone to enthusiasm and to discouragement" (687).

For Michaud, Mediterranean types were most importantly characterized by the fact that they "love art. The history of painting, sculpture, music, literature is mainly a Mediterranean history. France owes her present hegemony in art to the Mediterranean race" (687). Michaud argued that the influx of immigrants would supply, especially, those philosophical tendencies lacking in the American context: "a greater love for abstract knowledge, for the *science pure* of the French" (689). Too, the nation would benefit from "the artistic temperament of our Mediterranean friends" (689). Although that would mean "a decline of that enterprising spirit which has been called the American push" (688), he argued that the "marriage" of the Baltic with the Alpine/Mediterranean would be beneficial, for "we need every one of the qualities of the two alien races" (689).

Franklin Giddings, a sociologist whose comments on Michaud's piece follow, concurred. Acquiescing somewhat regretfully to the fact that "our blood will in part be other than English blood" (690), he still hailed the notion that "the American population is henceforth to contain a smaller proportion of the energetic Baltic blood and a larger proportion of the art and leisure loving Mediterranean blood" (691). Along with other Anglo-American assimilationists, Giddings welcomed the genetic addition of alien stock on the grounds that it would contribute to the American gene pool, the domesticated, cultured, and hedonistic proclivities of which the practical Anglo-Saxon was much in need.

Such gender-based racialism was a distinct departure from the racialization of the alien that had occurred during the earlier part of the nineteenth century. An Anglo-Saxonism initially elaborated in Britain in the work of John Mitchell Kemble and Robert Knox had been taken up with alacrity in the middle decades of the century by writers such as William Hickling Prescott, Francis Lieber, and Francis Parkman (Gossett 90–97; Knobel 110). Within their texts, however, racial difference was not systematically constructed along the lines of gender. Although the superiority of native Americans, or Anglo-Saxons, was seen to be a function of their possession of definitively masculinized traits such as courage, vigor, enterprise, and perseverance, there was no corresponding attempt to feminize the immigrant. One has only to look to the characterization of the Irish, perhaps the most intensively racialized European group during the early and mid-nineteenth centuries, to substantiate that statement. The racial inferiority of the Irish was seen to manifest itself in largely non-gender-specific traits such as pugnacity, stupidity, and alcoholism.[5]

Any assessment of why the immigrant became feminized at the end of the nineteenth century needs to take into account that "intensive questioning" of native white manhood that many critics—including Gail Bederman—see as a constitutive feature of this period.[6] This crisis in normative masculine ideals has itself been traced to the fallout of economic restructuring in the realms of culture and politics. The reorganization entailed changes in the form of ownership of property, a decrease in the percentage of individually owned businesses, and a radical retooling of labor management and organization practices (Sklar 431). The increasing rationalization of the shop floor, most graphically evidenced in the adoption of Taylorist management procedures, was an integral part of the emerging Fordist consensus in which managers sought to simplify and de-skill labor processes formerly controlled by workers.[7] Workers delivered increasing productivity in return for a higher standard of living achieved both through the direct wage and through other income transfers such as Social Security, education, and various welfare programs (Harvey 135). Higher wages also facilitated the mass consumption on which the retooled economy depended. Accordingly, as T. J. Jackson Lears has argued, a widespread cultural injunction toward self-indulgence and engagement in leisure pursuits replaced a long-standing promulgation of thrift and self-denial as the transcendent virtues.[8]

Bederman has argued that these shifts collectively fractured the normative Victorian ideal of manhood. She lists such factors as the economic depressions that struck between 1873 and 1896 and the proportional decline in the numbers of self-employed middle-class men as helping destabilize "the dream of manly independent entrepreneurship" that had been integral to nineteenth-century conceptions of manliness (13). Concomitantly, the adoption of an assembly-line process that bound the body ever more firmly to the machine stripped the labor process of any lingering semblance of autonomy.[9] Further, she argues that the novel cultural mandate to satisfy one's desires through the purchase of commodities undermined a long-standing equation of "self-restraint" with manhood (13). At the same time, the suffrage demands of the woman's movement, coupled with the emergence of a new strata of professional women (the "New Woman") who staffed the state's nascent welfare, health, and education programs, further destabilized the gender template of the previous century (13–14). Accordingly, Bederman contends that "turn-of-the-century middle-class Americans . . . use[ed] race to remake manhood" (5).

In similar fashion, Donna Haraway's analysis of the end-of-the-century founding of Roosevelt Hall at the National Museum of Natural History links the conservationist desire that inspired its construction to the attempt to stabilize a white male hegemony seemingly imperiled by the "extraordinary change in the relations of sex, race, and class" (55). Haraway points out that a substantial component of that perceived peril was the eugenic challenge posed by the immigrants.[10] The racialization of the new immigrant along a gendered axis was important in buttressing this beleaguered Anglo-Saxon male ideal.

That contention is substantiated by a reading of one of the earliest postbellum texts to refocus attention on the alien menace: the Rev. Josiah Strong's *Our Country: Its Possible Future and Its Present Crisis* (1886). Josiah Strong was a Congregationalist minister who during the 1880s became an official of the Congregational Home Missionary Society. The publication of *Our Country* catapulted him to national fame as well as to the position of general secretary of the Evangelical Alliance for the United States.[11] His writings also circulated in Britain, where he traveled extensively to promote his ideas. *Our Country* went through 175,000 copies in the United States by 1916, with separate chapters published in a number of periodicals and magazines (*Our Country* ix). The chief librarian of Congress went so far as to opine that the "power of its message . . . compared in intensity with that of *Uncle Tom's Cabin*" (ix). Strong's text was conceptualized and published well before the immigrant's feminization became culturally pervasive. His work presages that gendering, however. His concern about the social and political consequences of unrestricted alien entry was magnified by his explicit anxiety about the ability of an increasingly refined and nervous Anglo-Saxon race to withstand those effects.

Strong's immediate aim was to elicit funds for the support of American home missions. He described a series of "perils" threatening the imperial destiny of

Anglo-Saxon Protestantism, including urbanization, the Mormon faith, a rapid, unevenly distributed increase in national wealth, and the exhaustion of public lands. But Strong targeted immigrants, specifically their propensities toward Romanism, liquor, and socialism, as factors impeding the Anglo Saxon race's mandate to "spread itself over the earth" (214). "Foreigners are not coming to the United States in answer to any appetite of ours," he warned. "The lion . . . is having the food thrust down his throat, and his only alternative is, digest or die" (57–58). Strong argued that only Anglo-Saxons capable of withstanding the onslaught of immigration would triumph in *"the final competition of races, for which the Anglo-Saxon is being schooled"* (213–14, emphasis in the original). That victory depended on whether Anglo-Saxons could, in turn, conquer their neurasthenic tendencies. Drawing heavily on the work of George Beard, chief theoretician of America's "national disease" of nervousness, Strong acknowledged that as Anglo-Saxon civilization advanced it was becoming more refined, hence more nervous and less vital. Despite the threat immigration posed to a highly nervous population, Strong ultimately refused to call for restrictive measures. Instead, he restated his faith in the millennial prospect of Anglo-Saxon imperial triumph: "Is there room for reasonable doubt that this race . . . is destined to dispossess many weaker races, assimilate others . . . until . . . it has Anglo-Saxonized mankind?" (216–17).[12]

In his vilification of the immigrants' Catholic and socialist affiliations, as well as in the certitude with which he asserted the race triumph of Anglo-Saxons, Strong recycled all three strains of nineteenth-century nativist thought. The text's contemporary resonance is revealed not only in its use of Darwin's theory to buttress his millennialist vision but also in its connection of neurasthenia to the issue of Anglo-Saxon global hegemony.[13] Bederman has argued that the turn-of-the-century preoccupation with neurasthenia was, in one of its aspects, a symptom of the culture's pervasive anxiety about masculinity. The disease of nervousness embodied and proved the truth of the widespread cultural perception that civilized manliness "led to delicacy and weakness" (88), in other words, to effeminacy. Further, as a species of gender disorder, nervousness was explicitly linked to the issue of race, because Beard contended that, as the most civilized race, the Anglo-Saxon was especially subject to effeteness and frailty (86). The American nation, the finest flower of Anglo-Saxonism, contained the highest incidence of neurasthenia.

While Strong resolved his fears about the incipient effeminization and decay of Anglo-Saxon stock by yoking a millennial faith in the imperial destiny of God's Protestant people to Darwinian theory, Anglo-American assimilationists attempted to achieve the same end by projecting that effeminacy onto foreigners. Strong recycled familiar stereotypes about the seditious, intemperate, and morally depraved immigrant and argued that the conflict with the immigrant would reanimate Anglo-Saxon virility. Anglo-American assimilationists went a step further in articulating race and gender. They construed the immigrant as a definitively feminized other, upon and against which the virility of the native Anglo-Saxon reappeared. Imaging the process of alien assimilation as a heterosexual union, the codependence of the two terms was elided in favor of a vision of a mutual complementarity.

Harold Frederic's novel *The Damnation of Theron Ware* (1896) helped elaborate this emergent narrative. The text's thematic preoccupations bear witness to the gradual emergence of a discourse in which the alien's difference, signified via gendered categories, allayed fears attendant on a larger socioeconomic shift. Frederic was a journalist and novelist who, between 1884 and 1889, lived in Britain, where he was posted as chief London correspondent for the *New York Times*.[14] As Scott Donaldson notes, the novel was "greeted by reviewers . . . as 'a literary event of great importance'" (Frederic, *Damnation* xvii) and was critically acclaimed. It was also an immediate popular success in both America and England. It was singular for its representation of a wealthy and cultivated Irish immigrant, the beautiful Celia Madden, whose accomplishments render her the chief luminary of, rather than exception to, the Irish Catholic community of Octavius where she resides. What is notable, however, is the text's continuities with the larger cultural transition toward a new form of anti-immigrant animus. The novel evinces manifold anxieties about the individual and national consequences of the newly feminized presence of the immigrant that clearly dovetail with those of Ripley and Michaud.

The narrative traces the intellectual and sexual seduction of Theron Ware, an idealistic if somewhat naive Methodist minister, by Celia. Theron, newly posted to Octavius in upper New York State, discovers to his discomfiture that his congregation cleaves closely to "the old, simple, primitive Methodism of Wesley" (28). Brother Pierce, a trustee of the church, admonishes Ware shortly after his arrival in Octavius, "We stick by the Discipline an' the ways of our Fathers in Israel. No new-fangled notions can go down here. Your wife'd better take them flowers out of her bunnit afore next Sunday" (27). This strict adherence to the letter of their discipline is symptomatic of the Methodist congregation's mental and spiritual shortcomings. Ware's attempt to infuse a modicum of intellectual substance into his sermons is rebuffed. "We don't want no book-learnin' . . . in our pulpit," Pierce reproves. "What we want to hear . . . is straight-out, flat-footed hell" (27). Ware, who had fancied himself something of an orator and a scholar, is increasingly stifled by his flock's insularity. At the same time, his congregation's close-fistedness keep him both penurious and aware of the ignominious fact that he is entirely subject to their fiscal whims.

Under these conditions, Ware is drawn to Octavius's large Irish community, whose intellectual broad-mindedness and hedonistic tendencies contrast markedly with the Methodists' provincialism and puritanism. The counterpoint between the annual Methodist camp meeting and the annual Catholic picnic demonstrates the differences between the congregations. The Methodists concentrate on matters spiritual, nightly battling with "satan at close quarters" (230) as they "sang and groaned and bellowed out their praises" (228). In contrast, the Irish gathering has a "suggestion of universal merriment" (235). Sounds of "dance music" and of "the playful squeals of . . . girls in the swings" drift upward from their camp (235).

Frederic also contrasts the spiritual and intellectual outlook of each congregation's elite. The priest, Father Forbes, is a philosopher and sybarite. Having become acquainted with him, Ware is duly invited to dine with Forbes and Forbes's closest friend, Dr. Ledsmar, an expert in Assyriology and a scientist whose experiments include replicating Mendel's findings.[15] After a lengthy and elaborate repast, Ware is shocked to hear the two casually allude to religion as this "Christ-myth of ours" and is treated to a disquisition on the overweening social necessity, above all, for the existence of religion. Later in their acquaintance, Father Forbes observes, to Theron's discomfiture, that the church "is needed . . . as a police force" (243).

The third member of this circle is Celia. Her father, a Connemara peasant who has achieved financial success in the wagon industry, has endowed her with an "independent banking account," and she uses her liberal means to pursue interests in music, art, and literature. Celia's cultivation and sensuality prove irresistible to Theron. The two strike up a friendship, and she admits him to her circle of intimates, where he becomes acquainted with intellectual and cultural realms hitherto unknown to him. He is introduced to Chopin and George Sand by Celia and to Renan's *Recollections of My Youth* by Dr. Ledsmar, and he eventually begins to "borrow . . . all sorts of books boldly . . . from the Octavius public library" (232). After some months, he finds himself able to "swim with a calm mastery . . . upon the deep waters into which Draper and Lecky and Laing . . . hurled him" (232).

The challenges to Ware's religious convictions accumulate as the novel progresses. Accordingly, Lisa Watt MacFarlane has grouped *Damnation* with a number of other turn-of-the-century U.S. novels, including Henry Adams's *Esther* (1884) and Lew Wallace's *Ben Hur* (1880), that "focus on the place of denominational or sectarian faith in a larger social context" (128). Similarly, Scott Donaldson sees the novel as an exploration of the "various forces that were threatening American religion . . . at the turn of the century" (Frederic, *Damnation* xviii). These forces include "rational skepticism, scientific determinism, fin-de-siècle hedonism . . . [and] pragmatism" (xviii) and are embodied in Father Forbes, Dr. Ledsmar, Celia, and Sister Soulsby. Less explicitly perhaps but no less clearly, Frederic's exploration of the parlous state of the Methodist church is also designed, through its contrast with its Catholic counterpart, to demonstrate the archaism of the anti-Catholic animus that dogged the Irish community in America throughout the nineteenth century.

Two particular figures had stood as emblems of the perils of unrestricted alien entry: the Catholic zealot, whose supposed primary allegiance to priest and church threatened the very basis of republican institutions, and the seditious, bomb-throwing anarchist (Higham, *Strangers* 6–7).[16] Each was a figment of the anti-Catholic and antiradical aspects of nativist thought Higham has identified as the two most important in nineteenth-century anti-immigrant rhetoric.[17] It was, of course, the Irish who figured centrally in the former line of thinking. Thus Frederic's narrative, simultaneously representing and bearing witness to the newly residual status of anti-Catholic rhetoric, relegates Madden's religion to the status of contextual backdrop to the alien incursion rather than a source of anxiety about it. The spiritual fervor of Frederic's Methodists and the secularism of the Irish form an ironic counterpoint underscoring the anachronism of nativist fears that Romanist religious allegiance would undermine Republican institutions. On the contrary, the text suggests that the vibrance of the Catholic church might be a valuable resource in reinvigorating the besieged mainstream denominations. Father Forbes, observing the activities of his flock at their annual picnic, concludes, "As the Irish civilize themselves . . . and the social roughness of their church becomes softened and ameliorated . . . Americans will inevitably be attracted toward it. . . . [and] it will . . . be modified by them" (243).

Frederic himself, as London correspondent for the *New York Times,* was a longtime champion of the Irish in their natal home. His interest in their struggle for independence led him to cover Parnell's negotiations with Gladstone so exhaustively that his American editor had to remind him of his mandate to cover general European, rather than strictly Anglo-Irish, news (Myers 53). Although at one point Frederic sought to persuade American readers to his pro-Irish political agenda by informing them that "the Irish immigrants to America are of the poorest classes" (Myers 51) and hence unrepresentative of the capacity for self-government that the Irish at home possessed, by the time he wrote *The Damnation of Theron Ware* his enthusiasm would also seem to extend to the Irish contingent in the United States. In that respect the novel reflects a general attenuation of anti-Catholic nativism in the final years of the 1890s, which, as John Higham has argued, occurred in response to the progressive secularization of American society and the ongoing assimilation of the Irish (*Strangers* 86).[18] Fittingly then, Ware's increasing familiarity with the Irish induce him to revise his earlier religious stereotypes of that group. Previously he had taken it for granted that "all the drunkenness, crime, and political corruption were due to the perverse qualities of this foreign people . . . [and] the baleful influence of a false and idolatrous religion" (48).

One might argue, too, that the novel explicitly delivers the Irish from that racialization to which they especially, of all immigrant groups, had been subjected in the nineteenth century. Of course, anti-Irish feeling was not solely orchestrated around the religious issues of the period; the response to the Irish was racist and racializing, as the work of Dale Knobel, Noel Ignatiev, and David Roedigger has shown. Knobel argues that the racialization of the Irish within late antebellum culture was singular in its intensity in comparison with other European immigrant groups, although it began to recede by the 1880s. In that decade, conceptions of the Irish as mentally and morally stunted, conceptions linked in the writing of Anglo-Saxonists such as Robert Knox to Irish racial inferiority (Knobel 109), began to dissipate as "arguments for the inclusion of Irish Celts in the core blood group of the American nation" began to hold sway (176).[19] Accordingly, Frederic gives Theron occasion to renege on his racial stereotypes of the Irish. It occurs upon his first glimpse of Celia:

> He had never before had occasion to formulate, even in his own thoughts, this tacit race and religious aversion in which he had been bred. . . . The foundations upon which its dark bulk reared itself were ignorance, squalor, brutality, and vice. Pigs wallowed in the mire before its base, and burrowing into this base were a myriad of narrow doors each bearing the hateful sign of a saloon, and giving forth from its recesses of night the sounds of screams and curses. Above were sculptured rows of lowering, ape-like faces from Nast's and Keppler's cartoons, and out of these sprang into the vague upper gloom—on the one side, lamp posts from which negroes hung by the neck, and on the other gibbets for dynamiters and Molly Maguires. (48–49)

Depicting the Irish as cultured and urbane, and describing Ware's increasing attraction to all they represent, can be seen as a product of the reclamation of the Irish for whiteness within the nation at large.[20]

The text's treatment of race emerges as far more complicated than that, however. Frederic's representation of the Irish, although delivering them from the stereotypes elaborated by Knox et al., re-racializes them within the terms of an emergent discourse in which gendered traits are germane. Frederic's novel, like the texts of Ripley and Michaud, presents the immigrant as an aesthete and hedonist who values the life of the mind and the pursuit of leisure above all. Ware's intimacy with the Irish helps broaden his cultural and intellectual horizons immeasurably, replicating Michaud's arguments about the ameliorating effect on American life of the alien's "artistic temperament" and "greater love for abstract knowledge" (689). Because such proclivities are rigorously gendered within the terms of this racial schema, the Irish men in the book are all effeminate. Father Forbes wears his house-gown "with the natural grace of a proud and beautiful belle" (67), and Celia's half-brother Theodore has "prettily curling black hair, large, heavily fringed brown eyes, and delicately modelled features" (87). Celia's full brother, Michael, is "kindly, and simple" (86) and "displayed no inclination to marry" (87). He spends most of the novel succumbing to consumption and is given a Little Eva–like deathbed scene that retroactively confirms both his saintliness and his femininity.

It is Celia, however, freethinker and aesthete par excellence, who serves as principal mouthpiece for Frederic's views concerning the sociocultural impact of immigrants. In an early conversation with Theron, she describes herself as "an out-and-out Greek" (99), later declaring, "I divide people up into two classes, you know—Greeks and Jews" (194). Delighted with the speed with which Theron is jettisoning his Methodist tenets, she remarks, "You are getting on. . . . We are Hellenizing you at a great rate" (197).

In these passages, as Myers has pointed out, Celia is regurgitating ideas from Matthew Arnold's *Culture and Anarchy*. Arnold argued that the English cultivation of Hebraic traits led society to devalue cultured pursuits and the life of the mind. He defined "Hebraic traits" as proclivities toward "self-conquest . . . following not our own individual will, but the will of God" (113). What had been sacrificed in the process was Hellenism, which aims at "sweetness and light. . . . to see things as they are . . . in their beauty" (115–16). Hellenism, in short, exalts culture, the intellect, and aesthetics. Arnold also maintained that America, like England, was a predominantly Hebraic nation: "From Maine to Florida, and back again, all America Hebraises" (xxi). Arnold's schema is, of course, rooted solidly in Anglo-Saxon ideology.[21] "Science has now made visible to everybody the great and pregnant elements of difference which lie in race," he asserted, "that likeness in the strength and prominence of the moral fibre, which . . . knits . . . the genius and history of us English and our American descendants across the Atlantic, to the genius and history of the Hebrew people" (124–25).

In his attempt to reclaim the Irish for American citizenship, Frederic employed an Arnoldian theory that has a hierarchy of racial difference organized along a gendered axis inscribed as its first premise. Frederic's novel can hardly be said to record the definitive deliverance of the Irish from racialization. Rather, it reracializes them in accordance with that larger discourse of Anglo-American assimilationism whose contours I have discussed. Frederic, like Ripley and Michaud, welcomed the feminized immigrant influx for its potential to bestow the benefits of culture upon an overly practical Anglo-Saxon nation.

That articulation was, however, always particularly susceptible to destabilization. Indeed, at one point in *The Races of Europe,* William Ripley admits, "Far be it from us to assume that these three races of ours ever . . . existed in absolute purity. . . . No sooner has heredity set itself to perpetuating [distinct varieties of men] . . . than chance variation, migration, intermixture, and changing environments . . . begin to efface this constructive work" (111). The attempt to separate the races, to assert the binary logic of self and other, collapses, announcing its impossibility in the very effort to impose it. Such an implosion threatens the return of the effeminacy assimilationists had managed through displacement onto the alien; their narratives are haunted by the possibility that the immigrant's effeminacy would debilitate rather than complement an Anglo-Saxon host whose virility was already under strain from the impress of modern civilization. Examination of their work yields evidence of an incipient restrictionist position. Ripley himself, although stopping short of an outright call for an immigrant embargo, moved ever closer to it. In 1908, nine years after the publication of *The Races of Europe,* he compared Britain's "white man's burden" in India and Africa with what he called the "Anglo-Saxon's burden," a peculiarly American responsibility "to nourish, uplift, and inspire all these immigrant peoples of Europe" ("Races" 759). Failure in such a project raised the specter of race suicide, the prospect of "the Anglo-Saxon stock be[ing] physically inundated by the engulfing flood" (759).

Harold Frederic, too, despite his application of Arnold to the American scene, was far from sanguine about the impact of immigration thereon. That he was not impervious to the appeal of the rhetoric of exclusion is evidenced in an unpublished article he wrote shortly after 1885: "Closing the Gates."[22] The piece, intended for a British readership, details the history of U.S. immigration policy up to the passage of the Contract Labor Law of 1885 and attempts to identify the origin of the American public's anti-immigrant feeling.

In "Closing the Gates," Frederic's attitudes toward immigration uncritically reflect popular anti-immigrant prejudice. Citing lunacy, pauperism, drinking, and the spread of slums and socialism as being among the evils wrought by immigrants, Frederic excoriated, "The ignorance and chronic pauperism being tossed upon our shores by every heave of the Atlantic tide. No legislative skill or social barrier could prevent this evil leaven, once admitted, from working its way into the veins of the body politic" (5). By the time Frederic wrote *Damnation,* that hostility had not disappeared. The narrative's gendering of the Irish is attended by a manifest uneasiness. The novel contains less than muted anxiety about the sociocultural impact of those very immigrants it attempts to reclaim for American citizenship. Yet the complexion of Frederic's animosity has undergone a marked shift. The novel is pervaded by the theme of Anglo-Saxon decline, a degeneration both manifested in and symbolized by Theron's progressive effeminacy.

Lisa MacFarlane has performed a convincing reading of this effeminacy. Observing that "Theron has begun to figure himself as female, to see himself as the female to both Celia and Forbes" (137), she contends that Frederic uses his protagonist's gender ambiguity to examine the attenuated power of the ministry in a rapidly secularizing nation. Ware, she argues, is trapped "between his professional 'feminized' self and the self socialized as a man, [un]able . . . to negotiate . . . the ambiguous position of the minister in a heterogenous and increasingly secularized dominant culture" (130). Undeniably, the minister's effeteness provides a convenient device for exploring the shifting relations between religious and patriarchal authority at the end of the nineteenth century. What must be added to any discussion of Ware's gender ambiguity, however, is that it is triggered and subsequently exacerbated by his contact with the Irish. His increasingly ambivalent gender identification also suggests that the Irish community's dangerous influence no longer inheres in its alcoholic propensities or its chronic pauperism but in its contagious effeminacy.

Frederic raises the theme of racial degeneration in his opening chapter when he describes the gradual deterioration in physiognomy discernible across the several generations of Methodist ministers present at the annual Methodist conference. The worn yet noble visage of the oldest group conjures up memories of a time when "preachers . . . gave their lives . . . to the danger and wearing toil of itinerant missions through the rude frontier settlements" (2). The next-youngest group of ministers "looked like . . . honest and prosperous farmers. . . . The effect of these faces . . . was toward goodness, candor, and imperturbable self-complacency rather than learning" (3). In the youngest attending, however, the decline in "impress of zeal and moral worth . . . was peculiarly marked" (3).

If Frederic uses the devolution of the Methodist church as an analogue for the deterioration and softening of the native American type as its civilization advanced, Theron Ware appears to be an anomaly. His features are "moulded into that regularity of strength which used to characterize the American Senatorial type . . . before the [Civil] War" (6). His pedigree, however, is simultaneously proved and undone by his neurasthenic tendencies.[23] Theron has several nervous collapses. The first occurs during the opening ceremony of the Methodists' revival meeting, after which he spends the next few days in bed to restore his nerves. The second, more critical, breakdown occurs after Celia decisively severs their relationship. Subsequently, he is, in accordance with the best neurasthenic advice, packed off to revitalize himself "in th[e] . . . remotest West" (343).[24] The novel closes with Theron bound for the superintendency of a land company in Seattle.

Ware's initial encounter with Celia, the chief agent of his demise, occurs among the slums of the poorer Irish in Octavius. It is described as follows: "Presently he saw enter through the sunlit street doorway a person of a different class. The bright light shone for a passing instant upon a fashionable flowered hat, and upon some remarkably brilliant shade of red hair beneath it" (41). Her introduction against the backdrop of more normative nineteenth-century representations of Irish women—"before one of a half dozen shanties. . . . A stout middle-aged, red-armed woman . . . stood waiting. . . . There were whimpering children clinging to her skirts" (40)—alerts both Theron and the reader to Celia's distinctiveness. For Theron, it is not only her beauty but also her class that allows him to overcome his entrenched racial prejudice so quickly. As the narrator acidly remarks, the "glamour of a separate bank-account shone upon her" (254). It is that bank account that enables Celia's emotional and financial independence and empowers her to be a prototypical New Woman. Upon repeated occasions she expresses her feminism, as in a passage where she avows her refusal to marry: "That is the old fashioned idea . . . that women must belong to somebody, as if they were curios, or statues, or race-horses. . . . What on earth is it to me that other women crawl about on all-fours, and fawn like dogs on any hand that will buckle a collar on to them?" (254–55). The convergence of immigrant and new woman in the person of Celia yields clear evidence that anxieties attendant on the fracturing of normative Victorian gender ideals are implicated in the assimilationists' feminization of the immigrant.

Theron's manhood, already under pressure from an increasingly refined civilization, is gradually destroyed by his contact with the Irish. As he becomes besotted with Celia, he grows more and more effeminate. His intellectual awakening, according to the narrator, "softened bodily as well as mental fibres" (232), and his philosophical ruminations are compared to the flirtations of a woman. He plays with thoughts as "a woman of coquetry might play with as many would-be lovers" (232). He acquires the habits of a fop, purchasing a "shining tall hat," an overcoat with a silk lining (232), and a book "which treated of the care of the hand and the finger-nails" (232). Even more alarmingly, he begins to visualize himself in feminine terms. Desiring beer at the Catholic picnic but unable, as a Methodist minister, to purchase it, he wonders if "someone would bring him out a glass, as if he were a pretty girl" (236). This effeminacy both signals and manifests his increasing moral depravity. He begins to suspect his wife of the very infidelity that he mentally commits daily with Celia, and by the end of the novel his face has undergone a change from that of "saint" to that of a "barkeeper" (298).

Theron's introduction to music and Benedictine proves especially disastrous; the effect of such stimulants were believed to be particularly debilitating to a nervous personality. He encounters both during an audience with Celia in her private quarters. Upon entering the chambers, Celia acquaints Ware, in quick succession, with tobacco, Benedictine, and Greek philosophy, moving to complete her seduction and secularization of him with a virtuoso and particularly sensuous rendition of "that strange foreign thing," Chopin's Sixteenth Mazurka. It marks the precipitating moment of Ware's "damnation"; after that point his degeneration progresses rapidly. Appropriately enough, given the text's equation of native Anglo-Saxon decline with a failure of masculinity, the scene is also an Oedipal one. To reach Celia's quarters, located in the recesses of her father's house, Ware and Celia must pass through a series of doors concealed by curtains. Upon the threshold of the last of these, Celia turns to the minister and, holding up a candle so that "its reddish flare rounded with warmth the creamy fullness of her chin and throat," declares, "Now I will show you what is my very own" (190).

Ware, however, refuses to embark on the normative Oedipal progression. Dazzled by Celia and her piano playing, he ignores the insistent clues of the chambers' female statuary, which have "arms broken off, [and] was decently robed from the hips downward" (195). Mesmerized by the presence of Celia, Theron disavows the knowledge of the constitutive lack that is her "very own." Substituting her beauty and music for the missing phallus everywhere announced in the broken statues, he fetishizes the "glowing nimbus of hair" (199) and "the mingled delicacy and power of the bared arm" (202). The narrator repeatedly draws attention to what Theron ignores. Celia takes on "the posture of that armless woman in marble he had been studying" (198), while later, upon Theron's exit, she executes a triumphant "pirouette in front of the gravely beautiful statue of the armless woman" (203). Theron's refusal to recognize Celia's castration and the fact of sexed difference leads to his increasing effeminacy after this point. The progressive degeneration of his character proves the wisdom of Michael Madden, who, alarmed at Ware's constant attention to his sister, had admonished him to "keep among your own people, Mr. Ware" (298).

The race-gender articulation accomplished in the work of the Anglo-American assimilationists ultimately set the discursive stage for the emergence of a full-blown nativist argument. Madison Grant's *The Passing of The Great Race* (1916) brought Ripley's distinctions to the attention of a wider audience and yoked them to a nativist agenda (Gossett 354–55; Higham, *Strangers* 155). For Grant, as with Ripley, an Alpine is "submissive to authority . . . inferior in bodily stamina to . . . the Nordic," while again, like Ripley, he argued, "In the field of art the superiority of the Mediterranean race 'is unquestioned'" (in Gossett 355). Of course, Grant, along with his nativist peers, used such distinctions to argue explicitly for the exclusion of the new immigrant.

Thus Grant, like all nativists, sought to reveal that the differences elaborated by Ripley and others were signs of a latent and pervasive degeneracy. Such traits gestured to a larger and abhorrent racial difference, which, although occluded, was contained within the blood or plasm. Walter Benn Michaels has demonstrated that racial difference in this period became relocated from physical features to character traits. Race became viewed, he argues, as a matter of internal essence. Rather than announcing itself boldly on the surface, the attempt to establish the racial other as such drew heavily on the idea of hidden degeneracy. He writes: "As 'white' becomes an adjective describing character instead of skin, the invisibility of race reappears" ("Souls of White Folk" 193).

If an immigrant's surface did not necessarily embody those degeneracies lurking within to threaten the Republic, if the European—on the face of it—could seem American, the task of nativists became that of exposing the gap between appearance and reality, repeatedly dramatizing it, and alerting others to dissemblers. In terms of my delineation of the relationship between race and gender in the reorchestrated discussion about immigrant restriction, a logical extension of Michaels's argument suggests itself: Those feminine attributes and aesthetic proclivities ascribed by Ripley to new immigrants would become, for nativists, a key marker of (pejorative) racial difference.

The fact that Theron fetishizes Celia's aesthetic and intellectual accomplishments suggests that he is damned, not only because he refuses to recognize that these talents mask a sexual difference but also because he disavows the fact that they mask a racial inferiority. The minister seals his own downfall because he refuses to recognize gender-coded accomplishments as the sign of an invidious racial difference. Within the logic of Frederic's novel, the decline of U.S. culture, as manifest in the progressive effeminacy of its population, can be traced not only to the presence of the effeminate alien but also to the native's refusal to racialize that alien. In other words, Theron is damned because he is not a nativist.

Within the writings of nativists such as Madison Grant and Henry Pratt Fairchild, the immigrant woman, rather than merely a feminized influx, would become central. Nativists wedded eugenic theory to Frederic and Ripley's schema, thus forging a "scientific" reason for emphasizing the immigrant woman, encapsulating within herself as she did the most atavistic element of each race. Eugenics facilitated the nativist move toward treating immigrant women, the "ur-females" of an already feminized race, as an even greater threat to U.S. masculine virility than their already feminized male counterparts. In Frederic's novel, trembling on the cusp of nativism, the representation of the immigrant woman portends although does not fully mirror that construction of the alien female as the compaction of her race's essence and therefore as especially noxious.

On the one hand, Celia is the agent of Ware's seduction and is consequently singled out from her male compatriots as particularly dangerous. Celia's Connemara peasant father, her brother, and the intellectually astute priest, although all effete, do not elicit the intense narrative anxiety that accrues around her. On the other hand, the multiple ironies and ambiguities of the narrative voice, which repeatedly draw attention to Ware's solipsism, hubris, and petty provinciality, imply that he is at least as complicitous as Celia in his own damnation. Consequently, to trace the definitive emergence of the immigrant woman at the center of racialist thought it is necessary to follow the work of nativists who mobilized Ripley and Michaud's categories and yoked them to a eugenic theory of racial degeneration.

2

Flouting the Racial Border: Nativism, Eugenics, and the Sexualized Immigrant Woman

> The anxiety that attaches to the figure of woman is that of a
> difference that escapes the discourse of containment.
>
> —Abigail Solomon-Godeau

NATIVIST WRITERS of the late nineteenth and early twentieth centuries deplored the seemingly overwhelming influx of immigrants. They envisioned the threat in spatial terms, as an "engulfing flood" (Ripley, "Races" 759) and an erstwhile "trickle . . . [now] swell[ed] to portentous proportions" (Fairchild, *Melting Pot* 107). Lothrop Stoddard's *The Rising Tide of Color against White World Supremacy* (1920) presented a picture of the white world under siege from the nonwhite, with "frontiers," "dikes," and "gates" to be guarded. Within the "'inner' dikes" (226), too, the white man's resistance to "the rising tide of color" beating at his gates was being weakened by immigration: "When the enormous outward thrust of colored population-pressure bursts into a white land, *it cannot let live* but automatically crushes the white man out" (274, emphasis in the original). For E. A. Ross, "The melancholy spectacle of this pioneer breed being swamped and submerged by an overwhelming tide of latecomers from the old-world hive" (282) seemed, in the absence of some kind of legislative restriction, inevitable.

The shift in the newcomers' natal origin, coupled with their sheer volume, made nativists especially pessimistic about the nation's ability to successfully assimilate these new immigrants. Close to nine and a half million individuals from Southeastern Europe alone arrived between 1873 and 1910, and nativists never tired of repeating those statistics with due alarm (Persons 8). The destination of the foreigners was equally troubling: They converged on the cities and appeared to eschew those rural areas where immigration had characteristically tended (Persons 16).

Nativists were appalled at the consequent extension of immigrants' living quarters.[1] They envisioned tenement regions, with their alien inhabitants, as a fifth column ensconced within the heart of Anglo-Saxon territory.[2] For Stoddard, "The Nordic native American has been crowded out . . . by these swarming, prolific aliens and . . . in many of our urban areas [has] become almost extinct" (165). Ross worried that the substitution of streetcars for private cabs would have "the effect [of] . . . a narrowing of the esthetic space between those with position and those without" (in Kern 193)—in other words, between his patrician peers and that teeming mass of immigrants whose deleterious national influence he chronicled in *The Old World in the New* (1913).

Nativists repeatedly warned fellow citizens of the peril threatening native, Anglo-Saxon stock. From the early years of the 1890s, writers including Henry Cabot Lodge and Francis Walker used publications such as *Century Magazine, North American Review,* and *Forum* to sound the alarm.[3] Their themes were taken up and elaborated in book-length form by sociologists such as Edward Alsworth Ross in the teens and Henry Pratt Fairchild in the 1920s and further popularized by patricians such as Madison Grant, Lothrop Stoddard, and Clinton Stoddard Burr. Their analyses were published by respectable houses, among them Charles Scribners' and Little, Brown.

Nativists constructed an image of the nation as the besieged "broodland" of the Anglo-Saxon race and presented the reproductive front as the critical arena of battle. They stressed the immigrants' sexual threat and underscored the link between aliens' putative fertility and Anglo-Saxon race suicide. They also used theories of miscegenation drawn from the science of eugenics in order to elaborate the specific nature of the alien menace. In Fairchild's *The Melting Pot Mistake,* the nativists' characteristic vision of a struggle to defend an inside space against external encroachment takes place at the site of the body. Racial mixture between Anglo-Saxons and other races is seen to produce a "mosaic of separate racial traits" in which "every separate molecule remains just what it was before the mixing took place" (119). In this narrative, the national conflict is conducted intra-corporally as Anglo-Saxon "germ plasm" is seen to wage a losing battle against the more numerous, less developed, invading plasms.[4] Ross, too, fretted that "the blood now being injected into the veins of our people is 'subcommon'" (285) and, like many of his nativist peers, warned of the "'chaotic constitution'" being formed in the United States by the wide divergences in "human varieties being collected in this country" (289). Both the internal space of the body and the external space of the nation were racialized in nativist discourse, with the American continent and the native American body constructed as Anglo-Saxon "homes" under siege from aliens whose continued containment was essential.

The nativist response to the physical presence of the immigrant can be viewed as part of a general Western, urban phenomenon of the time. The discovery of the bodies and sexuality of the working classes occurred in the late nineteenth century and was, as Michel Foucault points out, contingent upon a series of conflicts: "in particular, conflicts over urban space: cohabitation, proximity, contamination . . . prostitution and venereal diseases" (*History of Sexuality* 126). Along with such clashes, the need of heavy industry for a stable labor force led not only to the "granting" of a sexuality to the working classes but also to a whole technology of surveillance—schooling, housing, and public hygiene—in order to keep that body under control.

Foucault was referring to Europe, but during the postbellum period American social critics such as Samuel Royce had begun to concern themselves with the need to train and educate the working class, seeing such tasks as directly pertinent to the issue of race. Royce's *Deterioration and Race Education* (1878) sketches a program of practical education that would tend to counteract "race deterioration," an especially critical endeavor in the United States, where "a comparatively new soil and a foreign climate conspire against the exogenous white race" (9). The monitoring of the working-class body and sexuality was intrinsically tied to a racial imperative. For non-nativist writers, the surveillance of sexuality was an attempt to "reinforce the species, its stamina" (Foucault, *History of Sexuality* 147). Surveying the laboring classes, Royce reported that race deterioration "is patent . . . from the lesser development of the muscular system, the narrow chest, the pale face, the delicate constitution" (9). Hence he advised a comprehensive program of "race education" that would have the goal of "constitutional improvement of the whole man . . . effected by the training of the body" (76), leading inevitably to the formation of "a noble national character" (77).

For nativist writers, however, the "discovery" of working-class bodies was simultaneously a discovery that those bodies were racially different and unmitigatably inferior. Any attempt to improve tenement conditions or institute educational reform only promised to hasten the contamination of true American stock. Madison Grant warned, "Where altruism, philanthropy, or sentimentalism intervene with the noblest purpose and forbid nature to penalize the unfortunate victims of reckless breeding, the multiplication of inferior types is encouraged and fostered" (48). Similarly, Burr, addressing the efforts of progressive reformers to improve tenement conditions, wondered, "Why spend time and money in an attempt to amend poor stock, as it rapidly increases in numbers, when by keeping it out of the world's newly occupied territories its species could be kept from propagating unduly?" (169). The issue for nativists was precisely how to contain the aliens' sexuality and hence prevent the proliferation of "substandard genes."

Of course, it was not only immigrant stock that elicited eugenic anxiety. The larger eugenic movement inveighed against the reproduction of all "feeble" strains. Poor white stock was targeted because it was believed that "there was 'a gene, or combination of genes, for poverty'" (McCann 120). Henry Goddard's *The Kallikak Family* (1912) presented a highly persuasive case for the implementation of eugenic measures with respect to what were termed degenerate native whites.[5] Goddard traced the offspring of one Martin Kallikak and demonstrated that his (illegitimate) union with a "feeble-minded barmaid" had produced a line of criminals and simpletons (McCann 105). His marriage to a Quaker woman of good stock had yielded, by contrast, a sterling line of capable citizens.

As Carole McCann argues, the clear message of Goddard's tract was that there were "dangers involved in allowing the lower classes to reproduce the bulk of the race" (105). Within the work of nativists, however, the line separating fit from unfit stock tended to be rigidly racial. Indeed, many of the patrician authors of these tracts imagined the native working classes to be facing the same prospect of race suicide that menaced their own class fraction. Thus, writers such as Ross, Stoddard, and Brandt took up textual cudgels on behalf of the native working-class, forging a cross-class alliance in the face of perceived racial onslaught (chapter 3). One piece of evidence of that compact was Edith Wharton's *House of Mirth* (1905).

As critics have begun to note, Wharton's narrative clearly manifests eugenic concerns. Elizabeth Ammons has urged readers to consider the "actual, important presence of race as a category in Wharton's work" ("Edith Wharton" 68). Citing the immigration debate, she argues that the narrative of *The House of Mirth* is designed to "save" Lily from marriage to Rosedale (80). Ammons contends that Rosedale—the "invading Jew" (80)—serves as a lightening-rod for the narrative's apprehensions about racial pollution. In that context it seems clear that the relationship between the blue-blooded Lily and the native, working-class Nettie Struthers is also a critical one. In a highly charged scene toward the end of the novel, Nettie tells Lily about the birth of her illegitimate child and of her husband's unquestioning acceptance of this child of a former lover. Lily perceives Nettie's financially straitened yet emotionally rich life to be an ideal one: "The poor little working-girl . . . had found strength to gather up the fragments of her life, and . . . [had] reached the central truth of existence" (Wharton, *House of Mirth* 319). The usually caustic narrator seems to endorse this sentimental perspective. When Lily later falls into the drug-induced coma that leads to her death, she does so under the impression that she is cradling and protecting Nettie's child: "She did not know how it had come there, but she felt . . . a gentle, penetrating thrill of warmth and pleasure" (323).

The eugenic implications of the scene are clear: Lily's death helps safeguard the genetic future of both her own class fraction and that of Struthers. McCann points out that for the writer and readers of *The Kallikak Family,* the "feeblemind-edness" of Martin's mistress is proven by her willingness to give birth outside of wedlock. In Wharton's novel, such willingness does not mitigate against the native working-class white woman's election to heroic status. Rather, in the context of the narrative's concerns with racial purity and race suicide, it actively facilitates that election.

Within the nativists' schema, the immigrant woman occupied an especially complex position. While she functioned along with her male counterpart as a villain whose take-over of Anglo-Saxon space threatened the Republic's very existence, she was also singled out as a particular locus of eugenic concern. All of the principal nativist writers took up the especially pressing issue of the immigration of women, particularly their preeminent contribution to the problem of race suicide. Madison Grant returned repeatedly to the specific threat posed by female immigrants in *The Passing of the Great Race,* as did both Ross in *The Old World in the New* and Clinton Stoddard Burr in *America's Race Heritage.* The Dillingham Commission on Immigration, which delivered its magisterial report in 1911, devoted an entire volume to the eugenic issues raised by the immigration of foreign women.

The commission's concern was the outcome of two decades of fulmination by eugenicists such as Francis Amasa Walker and Robert DeCourcy Ward, whose essays appeared regularly in such forums as the *North American Review, Atlantic Monthly,* and *Century* from the 1890s through the first decades of the twentieth century. Their work repeatedly linked the reproductive capacities of immigrant women to the supposed decline in the native birth-rate. Even after the passage of the Johnson Bill, the immigrant woman remained a particular target of eugenic animus. In *The Alien in Our Midst* (1930), a volume coedited by Madison Grant and containing essays by noted anti-immigrant activists and eugenicists, the contributors return repeatedly to the figure of the immigrant woman, whose extant presence continued to bode ill for America's genetic future.

Nativists drew upon the work of contemporary biologists that stressed the primary role of the woman in reproduction. Scott Nearing and Nellie Nearing, drawing on the work of Havelock Ellis, G. Stanley Hall, and others, summarized these biological arguments succinctly: "Racial qualities . . . are contributed to the race primarily by woman" (11–12). "'Woman is the race,'" they also observed. "She is less specialized, hence nearer to race type, more typical of the race, and therefore prepared to transmit to future generations the characteristics of the race to which she belongs. To woman primarily the race must look for its biologic progress" (17). Nativists took this scientific conception of the female sex and applied its tenets to the role of the immigrant woman. The work of Madison Grant and Clinton Stoddard Burr in particular construed her body as the primary bearer of inferior genes and presented her as the most dangerous element of an incoming "alien tide."

In *The Passing of the Great Race,* Grant began his discussion of the problem of immigrant women by summarizing these biological truisms and used the female's purported atavism to pinpoint the immigrant woman's central role in the racial struggle: "Women in all human races, as the females among all mammals, tend to exhibit the older, more generalized and primitive traits of the past of the race" (27). Accordingly, her propagation of racially degenerate progeny hastened the foreign take-over of native space: "If the conquerors are obliged to depend on the women of the vanquished to carry on the race, the intrusive blood strain of the invaders in a short time becomes diluted beyond recognition" (71). Ross, too, chronicled the critical position of the immigrant woman within the alien onslaught: "Township by township . . . the displacement of the American goes on—a quiet conquest . . . made by child-bearing women. The fathers forage, but it is the mothers who [wage] . . . the campaign to possess the land" (133–34). In similar fashion, Paul Popenoe, an eminent eugenicist, argued that "the principal danger [to Anglo-Saxon hegemony] would be the admission of non-homogeneous persons, particularly women, from countries with high birth rates" (213). And Burr, writing in 1922, was alarmed by the large number of foreign women who had "arrived since the Armistice of 1918" (180), stating that "in the past the rate of increase of the native stock has kept pace with the foreign stock only because of the disproportionate number of males, and the scarcity of women . . . among most of the elements of our immigration" (181).

Along with this construal of the immigrant woman as "nearer to race type" and thus the critical repository of retrograde genes, nativists imputed to her a preternatural fecundity. Whereas Royce had been alarmed by what he perceived as the tendency of tenement conditions to attenuate immigrant women's fertility, by the turn of the century writers of diverse political persuasions claimed that alien women had particularly high fertility rates. Furthermore, they inversely related those rates to the low frequency of childbirth among native Americans.[6] As W. S. Rossiter argued in the *Atlantic Monthly,* "It is obvious that the United States, in the face of ever-increasing reinforcements from abroad, has recorded a declining rate of increase and a decreasing proportion of children" (215). In 1911 the Dillingham Commission recycled this widespread assumption with its report, *The Fecundity of Immigrant Women* (United States Immigration Commission). By the 1920s, Burr perceived race suicide to be an established fact, although he consoled himself with the notion that, despite the fecundity of foreign women, "children of too early marriages (such as often prevail among the newer immigrant element) are apt to be of poor quality" (124). After the implementation of the 1924 immigration restriction bill (the Johnson-Reed Act), some nativists remained concerned with the extant presence of degenerate stock. They placed hope for the continued dominance of the Anglo-Saxon on the fact that "high fecundity declines rapidly under American conditions. The daughter of an immigrant woman bears on an average at least one child less than did her mother" (Popenoe 211).

The immigrant woman's sexuality was not solely linked to the issue of prodigious alien multiplication and the resulting decline in Anglo-Saxon births: It also invoked the specter of miscegenation. Nativists combined assumptions concerning the female's position as racial avatar with eugenic theories claiming the tendency of the more "specialized" (i.e., Anglo-Saxon) gene to be canceled in an inter-racial union. That combination rendered the immigrant woman's sexual congress with the native American an especially alarming prospect. The only way to mitigate genocidal, inter-racial sexuality seemed to be sequestering immigrant women within tenements. But Fairchild indicated the inherent difficulty of localizing the alien woman's infection of the body politic when he anxiously pointed out that "the sexual impulse knows no racial boundaries" (*Melting Pot* 114). For Burr, too, inter-racial sexual relations and their damaging national consequence—"the swarthy white types will gradually creep into the higher stocks and a mixed race result" (174)—seemed inevitable.

The figure of the immigrant prostitute served as a lightening rod for these nativist fears. In the thirty years preceding World War I, widespread concern over the vice problem spawned a myriad of reform movements and tracts dedicated to its management and eradication.[7] The immigrant woman figured centrally in that discussion. As historian Egal Feldman points out, although several contemporary reports proved that immigrant women were, in fact, not dominant in the vice industry, the immigrant woman and the prostitute were often conflated during this period.[8] Fairchild observed that "the whole trade [of prostitution] is fundamentally an affair of our foreign population" (*Immigration* 335). He further warned that the practice of soliciting immigrant women for prostitution had led to "the introduction of various forms of unnatural vice, more degrading and terrible than even prostitution itself in its ordinary form" (337) and used the supposed tendency of immigrant women to become prostitutes to urge immigration restriction (335). Ross drew on such attitudes when, discussing the non-nuclear arrangements of immigrant domiciles, he argued, "[There is] no doubt that in some instances the woman cook of the immigrant boarding-house is common to the inmates" (238). Even Jeremiah Jenks, a relative moderate on the immigrant question, argued that "the most pitiful as well as the most revolting phase of the immigration question is that connected with the social evil" (62).[9] So widespread did this assumption become that laws preventing "the importation of women and girls for immoral purposes and their control by importers" were implemented in 1907 and again in 1910 (Jenks and Lauck 313).[10]

Within those nativist texts that deal with the specter of the foreign prostitute, fears about the uncontainable nature of the sexually excessive woman are shadowed by eugenic anxieties about racial "mongrelization." As Stephanie Bower has argued, the eugenic misgivings that the immigrant prostitute elicited were articulated through the rhetoric of contagious disease. Drawing on the work of contemporary venerologists, Bower has shown that immigrants were believed to be particularly susceptible to venereal disease (39). She notes that medical and popular texts alike conceived the immigrant prostitute's womb to be "a fertile breeding ground for germs passed from 'new' immigrants to upper-class Anglo-Saxon" (33).[11] Bowers also mentions one report that argued, "The immigrant woman furnishes a large supply to the demand [for prostitutes]" (Vice Commission of the City of Chicago 40) and contended that the "continental" system of restriction—which had previously guided Chicago's approach to the control of prostitution and had attempted to contain and localize the "social evil" within certain classifiable, "segregated" districts—had failed (4).[12] Prostitution had repeatedly expanded into residential districts, spreading "disease amongst innocent men, women and children" (4). Accordingly, the commission recommended that a federal bureau of immigration charged with providing "for the safe conduct of immigrants from ports of entry to their destination" (55) be established in each large city because "immigrant girls should not be left to private expressmen and cab drivers" (40).

The rhetoric of contagious disease served as a powerful emblem for the eugenic threat posed by the immigrant to the nation's racial well-being. Yet foreign prostitutes were not merely graphic symbols of the national degeneration portended by the alien influx. Biological theory concerning the genetic outcome of miscegenation combined with biological accounts of the female's particular racial atavism to render the foreign prostitute an active, especially dangerous, agent of that national cataclysm. Accordingly, for contemporary observers agitated by eugenic concerns, the figure of the immigrant prostitute, who appropriated the native woman's rightful place with the native man and moved with impunity across the "racial border," was a particularly alarming spectacle.[13]

Stephen Crane's interest in both prostitutes and immigrants has been amply documented. *Maggie: A Girl of the Streets,* his short novel exploring the milieu in which such denizens moved, was initially published in 1893, two years after Francis Walker's "Immigration and Degradation" had appeared in the *Forum.* Laura Hapke reports that Crane "interviewed them [prostitutes], toured and possibly patronized brothels, helped a known prostitute escape arrest, and entered a common-law marriage with a madam, Cora Howorth Stewart" (19). It is also well known that Crane made frequent forays into the slums of New York in order to collect material for his sketches and fiction. As "an avid student of urban vice," he "began roaming the theater districts and immigrant neighborhoods of the Bowery and the Lower East Side for material" during the fall of 1891 (Benfey 60). As Christopher Benfey points out, such incidents are told and retold in the critical accounts of Crane's work, buttressing the author's claims that his literary goal was to approach the "truth of life": "The 'nearer a writer gets to life,'" he averred, "'the greater he becomes as an artist'" (in Shi 225). And although *Maggie* was virtually ignored upon its initial publication in 1893, upon its reissue in 1896 it was roundly acclaimed for precisely its "refusal to sentimentalise" and "aggressive and pitiless realism" (in Shi 229).

Evidence concerning the genesis of *Maggie,* however, implies that a draft of the novel was completed while Crane was at Syracuse University, before he embarked on his much-touted ethnographic missions into New York ghettos.[14] Benfey proposes that *"Maggie* was less the result of Crane's experiments than their cause" (61) and argues that the novel clearly borrows its "urban texture . . . from Riis and from Methodist tracts about the evils of the modern city" (63).[15] Rather than reading the novel as a pioneering example of urban realism, Benfey suggests that it should be seen as the stuff of "hypothesis, speculation, dream" (63).[16]

In the context of the eugenic trepidation beginning to filter through the pages of the nation's genteel periodicals, however, the narrative's concerns appear less a result of Crane's psychobiography than a product and expression of this burgeoning nativist sentiment. The novel's subtitle—*A Girl of the Streets*—signals both Maggie's profession and the novel's preoccupation with location and mobility. The anxiety generated by Maggie's ability to negotiate the clearly demarcated boundaries that structure the narrative is symptomatic of the immigrant woman's position within the nativist corpus as a whole.[17] In other words, the authenticity of Crane's novel does not inhere in its reproduction of the texture of immigrant life in New York at the turn of the last century but in the fact that it recycles and contributes to an emergent eugenic narrative concerning the menace immigrant women posed to the nation's well-being.[18]

The depravity of Crane's Irish characters is evidenced both by their sheer proliferation and their failure to remain corraled within the space of the tenement. Throughout the novel, Bowery denizens seep inexorably outward from their tenement buildings to the alleys and saloons beyond.[19] They seem to have their most meaningful encounters on the street, escaping from the violence endemic in the home to a space of more fluid power relations outside. In chapter 1, convicts ooze from their prison: "A worm of yellow convicts came from the shadow of grey ominous building and crawled slowly along the river's bank" (3). In chapter 2, Crane describes at length the tenement region in which his story is to unfold. The Johnson's building extrudes its gruesome presence into the street, refusing to remain self-contained. "Long streamers of garments fluttered from fire-escapes" while "formidable women . . . gossiped while leaning on railings," properly occupying neither the outside nor the inside. The whole building gives off an almost palpable reek: "a thousand odors of cooking food came forth to the street" (6). The tenement exposes its dreadful humanity, the repulsive descriptions of its inhabitants evincing a barely concealed anxiety at the uncontainable nature of that bestial other. Christine Stansell has written of the horror evoked in middle-class observers by the failure of tenement-dwellers to respect the division between street and home, by their tendency to make the former an extension of the latter: "Their domestic lives spread out to the hallways of their tenements, to adjoining apartments and to the streets below" (*City of Women* 41). In Crane's narrative, the threat posed by these inhabitants' free movement from tenement to larger urban space is intimately bound to that racial beleaguerment evident throughout the nativist oeuvre.

Crane constantly emphasizes the proliferation of children in the tenements. The opening scene presents "a very little boy [standing] upon a heap of gravel" surrounded by jeering urchins and yelling, "Dese micks can't make me run" (3). In chapter 2, Crane sets the tone for one of his appalled descriptions of the region: "In the street infants played or fought with other infants or sat stupidly in the way of vehicles" and "a dozen gruesome doorways gave up loads of babies to the street and the gutter" (6). Here, the immigrant woman's abnegation of her "biologico-moral responsibility" (Foucault, *History of Sexuality* 104) for her children proves her monstrosity; the constant stress on "loads of babies" clearly owes to the general nativist paranoia exemplified most succinctly in Frederick Bushee's comment that "in families of this [Irish immigrant] kind children are born with reckless regularity" (30).[20]

In Crane's text, paranoia surfaces in a metonymic condensation characteristic of the nativist vision. The reeking tenement-building, "quiver[ing] . . . from the weight of humanity stamping about in its bowels" (6), with its slimy walls and dark corridors from which tumbles a mass of squalling infants, represents the dangerously prolific body of the immigrant woman.[21] The description recalls Grant's characterization of New York as a *"cloaca gentium* which will produce many amazing racial hybrids and some ethnic horrors that will be beyond the powers of future anthropologists to unravel" (92), but Crane's excremental vision explicitly genders that depiction. The mindlessly proliferating alien female spawning a myriad of racial throwbacks is the antithesis of the undefiled and seamless female body that figures in nationalist rhetoric for the Republic itself.[22]

In *Maggie,* the domestic "spread" of the immigrant family out of the tenement evokes a generalized anxiety about the proliferating nature of the racial other. It is the immigrant woman, however, with her physical passage through the tenement door and out into the streets beyond, who most clearly embodies that threat. Whereas Mr. Johnson and Jimmy (the father and the boyfriend of Maggie) are depicted as merely pathetic in their respective weakness and egotism, Mrs. Johnson is monstrous and bestial. Characteristically, she is poised at a threshold: "The saloon door opened with a crash, and the figure of a woman appeared upon the threshold. . . . Her face was crimsoned and wet with perspiration. Her eyes had a rolling glare. . . . In the frame of a gruesome doorway she stood for a moment cursing them. Her hair straggled, giving her crimson features a look of insanity. . . . With a wrathful snort the woman confronted the door" (28, 29). Mrs. Johnson refuses to be confined, constantly breaking the bounds of her surroundings—"she began to kick the door with her great feet" (29)—and making forays to visit public saloons, to appear in court, or to fight her neighbors. Her degeneracy is clearly visible in her physiognomy (it has a masculine cast) and character; both her anger and unprecedented bulk mark her as excessive and insufficiently feminine.

Crane's characterization of Mrs. Johnson as aggressive and unruly draws upon a tradition of representation of the Irish immigrant woman that dates from the antebellum period. As Dale Knobel points out, the characterization of Irish men as preternaturally violent, and Irish women as being equally prone to aggression, was common in nineteenth-century America. Knobel quotes Thomas Butler Gunn's characterization of Irish immigrant women as "Paddyesses, whose arms were only less thick than their waists or speech" (94). Thus, Bushee drew on stereotypes at least half a century old when he wrote that "drunkenness and disorderly conduct cause the arrest of the majority of the Irish women" (107). Continuing, he argued that "when one sees a man rolled down stairs by his wife . . . the air thick with dust and expletives, we know that his name is Pat" (114). Although many mid-century depictions of the aggressive Irish woman played to comic effect, Mrs. Johnson's refusal to conform to the sentimental ideal of womanhood racializes and demonizes her.

The cult of domesticity had always been an implicitly racialized discourse in that feminine sexuality, autonomy, and physicality, foreclosed with respect to white women, returned with a vengeance in the figure of black women. It should come as no surprise that nativist writers explicitly mobilized this cult in their attempt to racialize immigrant women. They needed to find a mode of representing the immigrant woman that could adequately convey their sense of the monstrous biological threat she posed to national integrity.[23] One way of doing so was to yoke the terms and assumptions of sentimental discourse to their representation of the alien woman and her domicile arrangements. Thus, in *Anglo-Saxon Supremacy* (1915), John Brandt argued that "the Anglo-Saxons are real home-makers," as opposed to Balkans, Slavs, Latins, and Irish (172). Among the latter, "Families of the same blood continue to live . . . in the same miserable hut, generally in one, or two, dark, dirty, dingy rooms" (172). As opposed to their racial counterparts, "Anglo-Saxon women have wonderful tact in arranging cozy-corners, dens" (173), and Anglo-Saxon men show their racial superiority and do their part for the national uplift by "protect[ing] the family with insurance" (173). Brandt concluded that the "Anglo-Saxon home is conducive to good morals" and that "Congress is home on a large scale" (177). By contrast, the foreigners' racial degeneration is evidenced in their tendency to congregate in "dirty alleys, in illy ventilated tenement houses" (176). The immigrant woman's lack of home-making skills was proof of her biological inferiority.

Brandt's rhetoric was but the most explicit account of the nativists' widespread deployment of the sentimental ideal to racialize the immigrant. The very size of Mrs. Johnson unfits her for domesticity. She "looms," has "huge hands," and is "rampant. . . . The mother's massive shoulders heaved with anger" (Crane, *Maggie* 7). Her heavy drinking bouts cause her huge bulk to swell even further: "His mother's great chest was heaving painfully. . . . Her face was inflamed and swollen. . . . She . . . was eternally swollen and dishevelled. . . . She swelled with virtuous indignation" (12, 17, 26). Mrs. Johnson's refusal of an organic connection to the home accompanies her refusal of a "biologico-moral" responsibility to her children. She continually destroys whatever vestiges of comfort still exist in the Johnson's squalid apartment: "With lurid face and tossing hair she cursed and destroyed furniture all Friday afternoon" (21). Her departure from the American middle-class paragon of motherhood is shown in her infliction of punishment on her son Jimmie. In a parodic inversion of the ideal of the gentle, nurturing mother who ministers to the hurts sustained outside the domestic haven, "She dragged him to an unholy sink, and, soaking a rag in water, began to scrub his lacerated face. . . . Her eyes glittered on her child with sudden hatred" (7, 9). Similarly, in her relations with her husband, she inverts the middle-class paradigm of marriage: "The wife put her immense hands on her hips and with a chieftain-like stride approached her husband" (8). In the ensuing fight, "the woman was victor" (8) and her triumph leads the husband to retreat to the saloon, where he echoes Jacob Riis's interpretation of one root of immigrant family problems: "Why do I come an' drin' whisk' here thish way? 'Cause home reg'lar livin' hell!" (11).[24]

Within the novel, Mrs. Johnson's refusal to remain sequestered within the space of the tenement and the depiction of familial chaos pursuant to the breakdown of gender norms reinforce the unassimilability of the alien in general. It is only by considering Mrs. Johnson in conjunction with her daughter Maggie, however, that the novel's debt to a resurgent nativism becomes wholly clear. Although Crane's novel is distinguished by the virulence of its enmity toward Mrs. Johnson, it is her street-walking daughter, Maggie, who poses the most audacious threat to Anglo-Saxon hegemony. Initially, Maggie is the physical and moral antithesis of her mother in every respect. She is presented as the archetypal melodramatic heroine, a role that entails "vulnerability and a kind of passivity" as well as "perfect goodness" (Grimstead 174).

Maggie seems to lack merely the correct environment in which she might come to embody the ideal of Anglo-Saxon womanhood as outlined by Brandt. Her spasmodic attempts to beautify her tenement dwelling indicate an innate domestic proclivity: "Some faint attempts she had made with blue ribbon, to freshen the appearance of a dingy curtain. . . . She spent some of her week's pay in the purchase of flowered cretonne for a lambrequin" (Crane, *Maggie* 20). Therefore, at first sight, Maggie seems an anomaly. How could such a gentle, attractive girl have come to find herself in the company of the Johnsons? Her small size, naiveté, and victimization at the hands of her seducer, Pete, are repeatedly underscored.[25]

Even so, although seeming to embody the ideal type of American middle-class femininity, Maggie is equated with her mother in two ways: through a similar spatial mobility and through a similar physical description. Maggie's accompaniment of Pete to the saloons, theaters, dime museums, and to the Central Park menagerie, where sexes mix freely, and the Variety show, where sexes and races interact, mirrors her mother's perambulations. It is also an intimation of her future career, because, as Stephen Kern has pointed out, "The emergence of the cabaret in New York . . . broke down barriers of class, sex, and race that had dominated the entertainment industry" (200). For that reason, such locales were initially anathema to respectable citizens. Maggie's progressive deterioration and drift toward prostitution can be charted by her promiscuous circulation within these public places. It comes as no surprise that, despite her initial innocence, by novel's end Maggie becomes a "girl of the streets." She is a prostitute, and her body becomes a site at which the separation of public and private disintegrates and commerce and femininity conflate.[26] In the discursive division of gendered space, moral order depends on preserving the home as a hermetically sealed private enclave that is metonymic of the unviolated body of the woman. Accordingly, the prostitute emerges as a powerful signifier for the breakdown of republican order. In Crane's text, the immigrant woman, as a figure who refuses the sentimental connection to the home and traverses the private-public split, is conflated with the prostitute.

Crane's narrative uses physical description to drive home this association. To return to the figure of Maggie's mother, the portrayal of Mrs. Johnson—with her disordered countenance, wild eyes, black hair, and masculinity—clearly owes much to contemporary popular representations of the prostitute. Sander Gilman's discussion of turn-of-the-century depictions of the streetwalker's physique is useful. He cites the analysis of Pauline Tarnowsky, a Russian physician, who traces the degenerating appearance of the "physiognomy of the prostitute": "The first fifteen prostitutes on her scale 'might pass on the street for beauties.' But hidden even within these seeming beauties are the stigmata of criminal degeneration: black, thick hair; a strong jaw; a hard, spent glance. Some show the 'wild eyes' . . . of the insane. . . . When they age, 'their masculine aspect . . . emerge[s] . . . the face grows virile, uglier than a man's . . . the countenance, once attractive, exhibits the full degenerate type'" (224–26).

Although it is the daughter, Maggie, who becomes a streetwalker, Crane displaces the physique of the prostitute onto the immigrant mother as though to suggest that she confirms the daughter's inevitable future. This physical comparison becomes pronounced in the penultimate scene of the novel. Maggie solicits a progressively more debased series of male characters in what is clearly a synopsis of her career as streetwalker. Her gradual degeneration is intimated not through a description of Maggie herself but through a displacement onto the men she solicits and who reject her: "A tall young man. . . . [in] evening dress. . . . A stout gentleman, with pompous and philanthropic whiskers. . . . A drunken man. . . . A ragged being with shifting, blood-shot eyes and grimey hands. . . . A huge fat man in torn and greasy garments. . . . small bleared eyes. . . . brown, disordered teeth. . . . His whole body gently quivered and shook like that of a dead jelly fish" (55–56). In this brief scene, Maggie is revealed to be not only the reflection of her sexual partners but also the reflection of her mother. As Jayne Addams Phillips puts it, "[Maggie's] physical beauty [is] so ruined that she is mistaken for her mother by a passerby" (Crane, *Maggie* xii). Streetwalking strips Maggie of her dissembling exterior and reveals the racial taint that had hitherto surfaced only in Mrs. Johnson.

Maggie poses a threat in that she is the exemplar of an independent and defeminized sexuality. As an immigrant prostitute, she compounds this sexual threat by invoking fears of miscegenation. Her free movement out of the tenement space and into "the glittering avenues" (54) for the purposes of sexual solicitation portends—if unchecked—Anglo-Saxon demise.[27] As a sexualized figure moving back and forth across the racial border, Maggie occupies a liminal position where the attempt to maintain not only a rigidly divided gendered space but also a rigidly divided racialized space fails. Crane's nativist conflation of the immigrant and the prostitute positions Maggie's body, violated on multiple occasions, as a threat to (and, paradoxically, as an apocalyptic metaphor of) the degenerated Republic. Her mobility augers the futility of William Ripley's pious hope that "even if the Anglo-Saxon stock be physically inundated by the engulfing flood, the torch of its civilization and ideals may still continue to illuminate the way" ("Races" 759).

Crane's novel, finally, contains the menace it has exposed: Maggie's suicide occurs in the penultimate scene. Her death, as Aida Farrag Graff has postulated, proves the impossibility of ghetto-dwellers attempting to escape their environment. It is also a reassertion of control and a recontainment on Crane's part of the threat Maggie's mobility has posed to Anglo-Saxon hegemony.[28] Furthermore, her grisly drowning recalls a number of contemporaneous narratives in which the immigrant woman's presence elicits a violence implicitly linked to her key role in the racial struggle. There is the more sensationalist, if equally melodramatic, death of the Swiss-German Trina in Frank Norris's *McTeague* (1899), whose husband bludgeons her to death. In the same text, the Mexican Maria Macapa's throat is slit after she has endured a series of progressively more violent beatings from her husband. Similarly, the bloody death by miscarriage of Ona, a Lithuanian, in Sinclair's *The Jungle* (1906) can be read as part of a discursive complex in which misogynistic violence is yoked to, and engendered by, eugenic anxieties about America's racial future. The emotional valence attached to fictional scenes in which violence or death attend the presence of the immigrant woman may have operated cathartically for a native audience already habituated, through immersion in nativist rhetoric, to fear the immigrant woman as toxic to the national health. Thus the tragedy of Maggie is that she can only redeem herself—and the country to which she has immigrated—by ceasing to be.

President Roosevelt and Ellis Island: Racial Economics and Biological Parsimony

The competition of races is nothing less than the battle of standards of living. . . . The . . . race with the fewest wants or lowest necessities will . . . inevitably supplant . . . [those with] a higher standard of comfort.

—Frank Julian Warne

As for the displaced, the Iliad of their woes has never been sung—the loss of homes, the shattering of hopes, the untimely setting to work of children . . . the turning of thousands of self-respecting men into day laborers, odd job men . . . and "hoboes."

—Edward Alsworth Ross

IN THE MIDDLE of his *Immigration: A World Movement and Its American Significance* (1913), Henry Pratt Fairchild momentarily interrupts a description of that dystopian vision of race chaos, mongrelization, and Anglo-Saxon decay ever-looming on his nativist horizon in order to recount an anecdote. It describes a visit made by Theodore Roosevelt to Ellis Island. Wishing to "observe the effect of a gift of money on an immigrant woman" (191) but hoping not to be recognized, Roosevelt slipped a $5 gold coin to a staff member, who it turn handed it to the first woman disembarking with child in arms: "The woman took the coin, slipped it into her dress and passed on, without even raising her eyes or giving the slightest indication that the incident had made any . . . impression on her" (191).

Fairchild's ostensible reason for reproducing the tale is to defend immigration officials at Ellis Island against charges that they used undue violence in their treatment of immigrants. Certainly, he admits, even a casual observer could witness numerous uses of excessive force on the part of the officials. He concludes, however, that the imperturbability of the immigrant woman in the face of such unexpected largesse demonstrates that "it would be a remarkable man, indeed, who could deal with a steady stream of foreigners, stolid and unresponsive to begin with and reduced to such a pitch of stupor, . . . without occasionally losing his patience" (191).

Whatever Fairchild's immediate rationale for the presentation of this apocryphal tale, the spectacle of the immigrant woman's appropriation of a windfall $5 piece cannot help but recall that other immigrant woman who, more than a decade earlier, had already rehearsed for the reading public the remarkable facility of immigrant women with respect to the accumulation of gold coin: the Swiss-German Trina in Frank Norris's *McTeague* (1899) evinces a similar financial serendipity when she wins $5,000 in a lottery. Fairchild's tale of an anonymous immigrant woman invites comparisons with Norris's narrative in one further way. Namely, Fairchild's sanctioning of a prospective violence against the serendipitous immigrant woman recalls the tacit approval of *McTeague*'s narrator of Trina's bloody death at the hands of her husband. Such continuities signal the narratives' common investment in nativist arguments concerning the ramifications of the immigrant influx on the nation's economy.

Nativists did not rely solely on rhetoric impugning the immigrant's genetics in order to foment a restrictionist disposition among readers. On the contrary, their work also presented a comprehensive financial rationale for an alien embargo. Two economists, Francis Amasa Walker and Richmond Mayo-Smith, initiated this line of argument in the early 1890s, and it was recycled in the early years of the twentieth century by Frank Warne as well as by Fairchild, Ross, and Brandt. The argument asserted the economically disastrous effects of the alien influx, and it did so by focusing largely upon the immigrant's role in the market place rather than on the shop floor. This economic discourse drew upon biological race theory in two principal ways. First, it linked the immigrants' fiscal habits to the phenomenon of native race suicide. Second, it argued that inherent biological traits rendered immigrants unable to function within an emergent market economy. In this discussion, the immigrant woman, in her capacity as comptroller of her family's purse-strings and its chief agent of consumption, emerged as a particular target of concern.

Disapproving nativists complained that immigrants held "the most extravagant ideas of what is coming to them. . . . *insist*[ing] on relief as a right" (Ross 243). That tendency Ross attributed to Italian immigrants particularly, describing it a form of "spiritual hookworm" (243). Equally, Fairchild's narrative invokes nativists' repeated charge that American businessmen were locked with immigrants in a nationally destructive compact, with both sides motivated by the sordid desire for financial gain. Nativists excoriated those industrialists whose wish for cheap labor involved them in agitation against immigration restriction and led them to "sell . . . our [racial] birthright for a mess of pottage" (as the subtitle of Madison Grant's *The Alien in Our Midst* phrases it). Mayo-Smith and subsequent nativist writers stressed the immigrants' tendency to work for cheaper wages, undercutting (native) workers' incomes. Warne cautioned against "the socially injurious and individually disastrous effects upon the American worker of this foreign stream of cheap labor" (*Immigrant Invasion* 279), while Ross argued that "the pouring in of raw immigrants has weakened their [the trade unionists] bargaining power" (208). Such reasoning had helped effect the passage of the Contract Labor Law of 1885, which forbade employers from prepaying the transportation of non-native workers (Higham, *Strangers* 48–49).

When nativists turned their attention to the economically deleterious effects of immigration, they did not abandon their racializing discourse. Indeed, for these writers, economics was inevitably and inextricably bound up with issues of eugenics and race warfare. Nativists argued that native workers, faced with decreased wages as a result of an overabundant foreign labor supply, were unwilling either to reduce their living standards or supplement the family income by sending their children out to work. They responded instead by reducing the size of their families: "William does not leave as many children as 'Tonio, because he will not . . . eat macaroni off a bare board . . . and keep his children weeding onions" (Ross 303). The decision to sacrifice family size in order to maintain living standards was, posited nativists, the root cause of that phenomenon dubbed "race suicide." Race suicide was manifest in the precipitous decline in size of native Anglo-Saxon families remarked upon by many cultural commentators. Such family planning was not, it was averred, practiced by immigrants. On the contrary, they were reproducing more rapidly in order to take advantage of the wage-earning capacities of their children. Thus, in Fairchild's anecdote, the figure of Roosevelt serves as a copula linking an explicit economic concern with implicit racial anxiety.[1]

Author of such tracts as "A Premium on Race Suicide" and "Race Decadence," Theodore Roosevelt was well known for his eugenic views.[2] In a letter to Charles Davenport (the intellectual leader of the American eugenic movement), he averred that "'the prime duty, the inescapable duty, of the *good* citizen of the right type is to leave his or her blood behind him in the world'" (in Pickens 120, emphasis in the original). In accordance with these beliefs, Roosevelt publicly exhorted American women to dedicate themselves to that "great primal work of home making" and child-rearing, a function that rendered her the "only indispensable citizen" (Roosevelt, *Theodore Roosevelt* 324, 323). Indeed, Donald Pickens reports that the president, alarmed at the supposed decline in native stock, personally wrote to a Mr. and Mrs. R. T. Bowen, "congratulating them for having twelve children" (124). That publicly assumed stance rendered Roosevelt the most prominent Jeremiah with respect to the issue of (Anglo-Saxon) race maintenance. He usually identified the "new woman" rather than the immigrant's depressive effect on wages as the cause of race suicide.[3] In 1901, however, Roosevelt recycled the views of nativist economists, describing foreign laborers as "represent[ing] a standard of living so depressed that they can undersell our men in the labor market and drag them to a lower level" (in Warne, *Immigrant Invasion* 307). Thus, Fairchild's depiction of Roosevelt observing a financial transaction with a newly disembarked immigrant yokes, by inference, the problem of race suicide to the economic effect of the new immigration.

The economic explanation for the decreased size of native families always contained latent within it a racialist argument. In the work of many nativist economists, the argument gradually superseded speculations about the effects of an abundant labor supply on the standard of living for natives and immigrants, the writer proceeding instead to implicate the foreigners' racial proclivities toward a "pigsty mode of life" (Ross 219) as the source of race suicide. Francis Walker's claim that it was the immigrant influx's "vastly lower standard of living . . . [and] incapacity even to understand the refinements of life" (641) that "constituted a shock to the principle of population among the native element" (640) set in place an argument to which nativists subsequently had repeated recourse: the idea that immigrants had a constitutional tendency, no matter what their income, to cleave to a low standard of living. Richmond Mayo-Smith sounded the alarm, too, arguing that immigrants "in former times . . . had the desire for a higher style of living. . . . In recent years, however, a class has come, accustomed to a distinctly lower standard, with no notion of anything else" (132). John Brandt recycled those claims, arguing that immigrant families of Balkan, Slav, Latin, and Irish origin "continue to live, decade after decade, in the same miserable hut, generally in one, or two, dark, dirty, dingy, rooms with a few ill kept articles of furniture" (172). And Ross's *The Old World in the New* presents itself as a valediction to the native working class, whose advanced evolutionary status and consequent demand for a high standard of living rendered them, ironically, the loser in the economic survival of the fittest.

An affinity for squalor was coupled with an ascription to the alien of a well-nigh pathological desire to accumulate savings, pathological because that feat often necessitated an extreme level of material deprivation. Nativists repeatedly indicted the immoderate frugality of immigrant families, which led them to sacrifice present well-being for the sake of various future contingencies (a tendency precisely the opposite of the industrialists, seen to be busily sacrificing the racial future of the nation for the sake of present material gain). Mayo-Smith targeted particularly the Italians, French Canadians, and Scandinavians as people who "economize in every way" (135) and cited a Professor Hadley, who opined of the new immigration, "In economy of food . . . they teach us a lesson from which we might learn a good deal. The trouble is that their economy does not stop at point where it would be desirable" (144). Two decades later, Ross described immigrants generally as "ignorant, avaricious rustics" (244) who saved too much. He showcased the Slavs, particularly, as an immigrant group who "'save so greedily that their children become disgusted with the wretched home conditions and sleep out'" (246). Frank Warne quoted a Consul Sterne on the subject of Slovak immigrants. Having recorded their gustatory predilection for offal, Sterne summarized: "In all, it will be seen that the tastes of these people are anything but refined, are low, in fact, . . . [they have an] ever present object to economise" (*Immigrant Invasion* 136–38). What began as an argument indicting the greed of entrepreneurs who used immigrant labor as a method of keeping wages low slid quickly, for all writers, into an indictment of the accumulative mania of immigrants that dictated that they remain in squalid domestic environs.

The construction of a racial parsimony as the cause of "low standards of living" for foreign families facilitated an important move in the argument of these economists. The tireless invocation of the immigrants' perniciously "low standard of living" raised questions about whether, in fact, they were capable of functioning satisfactorily within a market economy. Mayo-Smith, for example, suggested that "degraded [foreign] labor with its lower standard of living does not make the same demand for commodities that the old [immigration] did" (143). Employers' arguments concerning immigrant labor's net worth to the United States in terms of production of wealth rendered discussions of that labor's harmful economic effects less than persuasive, a fact Mayo-Smith, Ross, and Warne admitted.

Attention to the immigrants' constitutional miserliness enabled nativists to sidestep arguments concerning immigrants' contributions to the production of national wealth and to target non-native consumption habits instead. As Warne asserted, "We have not vindicated free immigration even economically, when we have shown that it increases the production of wealth" (*Immigrant Invasion* 143).[4] At the same time, the transition underway in the United States from a production-based to a consumer-based economy, as well the high degree of cultural awareness of that shift evidenced in the ongoing public debate about its nature and implications, allowed nativists to use aliens' putative consumption habits to foment a racial-economic resentment that had a specifically contemporary resonance. Thus, nativists targeted foreigners' consumption habits, or supposed lack thereof, when they set about forging an argument about immigration's disastrous economic effects.

Jackson Lears has lucidly described the shift in cultural mores that accompanied the transition from an economy of scarcity to one of abundance.[5] The "new morality" valorized spending, enjoined the satisfaction of ever-expanding material desires, and encouraged indulgence in leisure pursuits and other nonessential commodities. Previously hegemonic values of thrift, savings, and self-denial were deemphasized. In such a milieu, the innate parsimony nativists ascribed to immigrants put them at odds with the emergent consumer economy and its attendant morality.[6] Racially ingrained habits of frugality rendered them constitutionally unfitted to such a changed economic context. At the same time, however, the ease with which nativists were able to position immigrants as recipients of a cultural animosity in this respect betokens the displacement of a larger cultural apprehension about the ongoing economic transition onto the figure of the parsimonious immigrant. Lears stresses that the new economic morality did not instantly displace its forbear. Rather, the two coexisted in uneasy tension as residual injunctions to hoard warred with the new mandate to satisfy desires through consumption. The speed with which the putative frugality of immigrants became widely accepted, coupled with the hostility it aroused, suggests that the native's difficulty in extirpating a long-valorized thrift, even in the face of the myriad blandishments of the advertizing industry, produced the intensive return of that parsimony in the phantasmatic figure of the miserly immigrant.

Frugal habits were, however, destructive in ways that reached well beyond their retardant effect on the economy. Contemporary commentators construed the elaboration and intensification of the desire for consumer goods mandated by the new morality as vital not only to the continued growth of the economy but also to the increasing refinement of American culture—and thus to the continued development of its civilization. Simon Patten, one of the earliest economists to theorize about the implications of the economy's supposed deliverance from scarcity, linked increased consumption to continued cultural and national progress: "The first rapid advance [in civilization] has been made when the desires have been intensified and multiplied until men who are now content to live five days on the earnings of two can no longer make both ends meet. If they have few wants and less imagination, they may never improve" (127–28). Such ideas were widely disseminated, both by Patten and by his students. Clearly, construing the immigrant as constitutionally averse to consumption would, in the context of such arguments, buttress nativists' calls for their definitive exclusion.

It was, however, a difficult case to make because many contemporary commentators, Patten included, viewed consumption as an avenue whereby immigrants might be made over into American citizens. Patten explicitly presented the economic theory in his *The New Basis of Civilization* (1907) as a definitive rebuttal of nativist arguments concerning the negative economic and cultural effects of immigration.[7] His opening chapter refutes the arguments of those who "fear a lower wage and greater poverty as the bitter fruit of the throngs of eager workers who press into our ports" (11). The "discovery of abundance" rendered these fears untenable. Instead, he envisioned consumption as an avenue whereby "primitive" man, by which he meant both native working class and immigrant, would be effectively socialized: "Men must enjoy, and emphasis should be laid again upon amusement so extended and thorough that primitive people may be incorporated by its manifold activities into the industrial world" (143). Immigrants' consumption would not only fuel the economy but, equally important, would integrate and assimilate them into modern U.S. culture. Against those who pointed to the immigrants' sordid living conditions as evidence of their refractory refusal to consume, Patten countered with "the elaborated, unsanitary feather-beds which fill too much space in the Italian tenements . . . [and] the heavily embroidered gingham aprons" of the women (140). Both objects provide evidence of luxurious aspirations that can be satisfied by the consumption of commodities; in turn, buying would render immigrant women American.

Patten's ideas were widely shared. Stuart Ewen and Elizabeth Ewen have chronicled the contemporary faith in the "democratic" power of the market. They argue that the consumption of American goods, especially of American mass fashion, was represented to the immigrants by the industry itself as "one of the few avenues by which people could assume a sense of [national] belonging" (211). Similarly, Martha Banta cites an article in an 1896 issue of the *New York Journal*—"Who Is the American Princess?"—in which the market's assimilatory power was assumed. The newspaper counterpoised an image of heiress Gertrude Vanderbilt to one of Bowery girl Bertha Krieg, the message being, argues Banta, that "the aesthetic of the American Girl . . . can be copied by way of cheap versions of expensive clothes" (*Imaging American Women* 109). Immigrants themselves certainly understood the degree to which many native commentators perceived participation in luxury consumption as constituting both evidence of a desire to assimilate and an important medium of that process. In Anzia Yezierska's novel *Bread Givers* (1925), the immigrant heroine, Sara, gauges her family's progress toward Americanization by means of their increasingly sophisticated consumption habits. As she asserts, "And more and more we wanted more things, and really needed more things the more we got them" (29).

Nativists countered by constructing immigrants as constitutionally unable to adapt to a consumer economy. One of the earliest attempts to present their "refusal to spend" as an intractable racial characteristic was made by Nathaniel S. Shaler in the *Atlantic Monthly* in 1893. In an essay entitled "European Peasants as Immigrants," Shaler contended that the persistence of feudalism (a social system in which movement up the social hierarchy is impossible) in the immigrants' natal home "checked the development of all those motives and aspirations which are the foundations of our democracy" and bred "only one distinct desire," that of "more opportunities for gain" (649). Among these immigrants, however, even "the gainful motive" was "singularly limited. Money is desired for its own sake. The peasant who attains a fortune rarely alters his scheme of living" (650). Instead, a peasant who unexpectedly acquires wealth "becom[es] a true miser, in a way which . . . is impossible, in a democracy" (650). Shaler's arguments lead him to call for a halt to immigration because, although he linked the acquisition of miserly traits to the effects of a particular socioeconomic system, his neo-Lamarckianism led him to believe that these acquired habits would continue to appear in future generations. Such arguments were repeatedly made during the next two decades by Fairchild, Ross, Brandt, and Warne, all of whom continued to link deficient consumption habits to a biologically based, pathological thrift coupled with an innate propensity toward squalor.

Within this context, then, Fairchild's vignette of Roosevelt and the newly disembarked immigrant condenses a widely disseminated nativist argument concerning the impact of immigrants on an emergent consumer culture. The anecdote signals the arrival of a population who, tenaciously accumulating wealth but refusing to recycle it through consumption, worked against the needs and logic of the market economy. Furthermore the tendering of the coin upon the woman's disembarkation signaled her deliverance, upon her arrival in the United States, from an economy of scarcity into one of abundance. Her swift arrogation of the gold and deft dispatch of it to some invisible recess of her person augered its presumed fate, because the immigrant "often stuffs [savings] into his belt or under a mattress" (Kellor, *Immigration and the Future* 200). The immigrant woman's refusal to recycle the gold through consumption will not even lead to the generation of wealth through the alternative avenue of investment, for, as Kellor continued, "The world of investments . . . is unknown to him [the immigrant]" (200). By implication, the immigrant woman's appropriation of the gold coin will lead to a general lowering of living standards, an inhibited level of cultural development, and a native refusal to reproduce in such an uncongenial environment.

Within this vignette, one further fact needs to be adduced in order to account for the relevance of the newly disembarked immigrant's sex—the particular significance of woman's position within the emergent market economy. Historians have stressed the fact that woman's role as chief consumer for her family meant that under the changed economic conditions, "the organized effort of 'producers' to sell to 'consumers' . . . [took] the form of a masculine appeal" (Bowlby 19). Contemporary commentators repeatedly remarked upon the newly acquired function of women in their role as spenders. Bertha Richardson sought to bring readers to an awareness of that power when, in *The Woman Who Spends* (1910), she urged middle-class women to use their purchasing prerogative to reward those employers who maintained humane and hygienic factory conditions. Scott Nearing and Nellie Nearing emphasized the particular importance of a working-class woman's spending power: "Within a century, women have evolved from producers into spenders. . . . Among the poor, particularly . . . women direct the expenditures for consumption goods" (171). Sophonisba Breckinridge concurred, arguing that "the importance of the spending function of the housewife must be brought home more clearly to great numbers of women" (138). This contemporaneous and widespread perception of the importance of woman's consumer role within the emergent economy of abundance threw into relief the frugal immigrant female, whose constitutional reluctance to spend had a retardant effect upon the economy and upon the progress of U.S. civilization as a whole.

By 1921 concern about the parsimonious proclivities of the immigrant woman had become so widespread that Breckinridge, whose agenda in *New Homes for Old* was to argue the recuperability of the immigrant for the American (domestic) way of life, felt the need to directly and lengthily tackle the issue: "There has been in the past much harsh and thoughtless criticism of the foreign-born groups, because of the extent to which they have seemed able and willing to subordinate present necessities and enjoyments" (85). Breckinridge construed the foreign female's frugal tendencies as learned, rather than biologically based, behavior. She admitted that the immigrants' "thrift often seems to border on miserliness" (87) and that they have long cleaved to the "doctrine [of] *save first and spend afterward*. . . . giv[ing] rise to comment on the 'low standard of life'" (87, emphasis in the original). Breckinridge attributed such habits, however, to a variety of social conditions, including "unfamiliarity with money" (88), "irregularity of income" (91), and the need to put up "reserves for misfortune" (92). Presenting commodity consumption not as an innate facility but a skill or even an art, she suggested that "foreign-born housewives need, as most housewives need, instruction in the art of spending" (114). Thus, in a section entitled "The Neglected Art of Spending," she laid out a comprehensive plan of education for the immigrant woman in "the selection of food and clothing, and the variety of demands for which provision must be deliberately made in a modern industrial community" (114).

A similar concern to redress the widespread perception of the immigrant woman's innate miserliness is apparent in the work of Kellor, one of Breckinridge's fellow Americanizers. Kellor teetered on the verge of biological racism when she wrote that "thrift is . . . seen to be the companion of adventure in the new country [which]. . . . accentuates even the *natural* thrift of the immigrant" (*Immigration and the Future* 199, emphasis added). Yet in a previous chapter— "Foreign Markets in America"—she advocated "the education of immigrant women and children in the knowledge and use of American-made goods" (178) as an effective means of removing impediments to their successful integration into commodity culture.

Nativists refused to entertain the possibility that immigrant women could be retrofitted to function effectively within a market economy, and they returned repeatedly within their work to the figure of the immigrant woman as a harbinger of racial-economic disaster. Frank Norris's *McTeague* (1899) is a particularly unsubtle recycling of such representations. It would be hard to find a text in which the thrifty proclivities of immigrant women are more sharply foregrounded. Work on Norris's oeuvre has stressed its debt to the larger nativist discourse, and *McTeague* especially, like Stephen Crane's *Maggie,* derives a large part of its power from the exposure and containment of the racial threat posed by the immigrants who populate its pages. Jared Gardner has effectively sketched the novel's nativist logic, which mandates that "blood tells all, despite the characters' attempts to silence its pronouncements" (58). Walter Benn Michaels has paid close attention to the text's economic concerns. His *Gold Standard and the Logic of Naturalism* describes the novel within the twinned contexts of an emergent market economy and the ongoing cultural debate around the maintenance of the gold standard. The racial and economic concerns of the text are intimately linked, however. *McTeague,* like the economic texts of Mayo-Smith and Walker, delineates the cataclysmic effect of the immigrant presence on the national socioeconomic scene; considering the text in terms of that "racial-economic" aspect facilitates an understanding of the intensity of the narrative animus directed against the Swiss-German woman, Trina. Her contribution to the demise of her hapless husband exemplifies nativist predictions about the impact of immigration on the native working-class population.

Contemporary reviewers understood the implications of Trina's immigrant background well. A *Washington Times* reviewer described her as "a little Swiss girl" possessed only of a "half-developed civilization and strong ancestral and racial instincts" ("A Western Realist" 47). She, along with the other immigrant characters such as the Mexican woman Maria Macapa, is "full of half-understood racial tendencies inherited from Old World ancestors, veneered with a superficial intelligence and culture due to American institutions" and "hopelessly incapable of real refinement till at least three generations of them have lived, learned, and suffered in a free land" (47). Her racial "instincts," initially hidden, emerge gradually after she wins the lottery. The unexpected acquisition of wealth catalyzes an atavistic greed, which in turn destroys both she and McTeague.

McTeague functions within the novel as a representative native worker. Contemporary readers versed in racial typologies would have had little difficulty in discerning his racial descent from Norris's physical descriptions. In his review of the book, William Dean Howells referred to McTeague as "a massive blond animal" ("A Case in Point" 14), and Richard Chase has argued that McTeague is "of the confraternity of the blond beast, the 'Nietzschean' or 'Darwinian' Adam, so much admired by Norris and Jack London" (*American Novel* 191).[8] Norris describes him as "a young giant . . . carrying his huge shock of blond hair . . . heavy with ropes of muscle" (*McTeague* 3). He is one of those descendants of the "pioneer breed" elegized by Ross: an offspring of "Angles, Jutes, Danes, and Normans . . . a product of frontier life. . . . gritty, uncomplaining, merciless to the body. . . . even when . . . dirty, ferocious barbarians, these blonds [are] truth tellers" (289–93). Mats of blond hair cover McTeague's massive hands, and he demonstrates an outrageous strength and utter lack of physical cowardice. He has "the great blonde mustache of a viking" (*McTeague* 135–36), and his rage is described as resembling "the exalted and perverted fury of the Berserker" (234–35).[9] His brute strength and courage are coupled with a coarseness and stupidity that mark him as one of those primitive Anglo-Saxons who occur repeatedly in Norris's fiction. For example, his description recalls the Norwegian heroine of *Moran of the* Lady Letty, who is "massive" (71), "coarse-fibred . . . both mentally as well as physically" (72), and whose "neck [is] . . . thick, strong . . . her hands roughened and calloused" (104). Like McTeague, her strength goes hand in hand with a complete lack of refinement but like him, too, that "coarseness . . . would prove to be the coarseness of a primitive rather than of a degenerate character" (72).[10]

In that respect, my argument departs from that of Jared Gardner and Hugh Dawson, both of whom have argued that McTeague should be understood to have immigrant origins and to share in the narrative animus directed against Trina. They premise that supposition in part on the fact that one of Norris's sources for *McTeague* was a newspaper account concerning an Irish laborer named Patrick Collins who murdered his wife after she refused his request for money. The explicit physical descriptions of McTeague, however, coupled with an attention to the novel's continuities with Norris's earlier short stories that chronicle the destruction of Anglo-Saxon males by foreign females—"A Case for Lombroso" (1897) and "After Strange Gods" (1894)—make such a reading untenable. Norris strips his character of the source's immigrant origins. Thus, he is able to demonstrate the catastrophic effect of the immigrant's racial-economic traits on a primitive type of native worker who has only recently been introduced into an urban, consumer culture.[11]

Residual anxieties concerning the socioeconomic repercussions of the immigrant presence are given early and explicit expression in Norris's text. McTeague's friend Marcus Schouler inveighs against the capitalists' and immigrants' joint conspiracy to undo native workers' wages: "Decrease the number of wage earners and you increase wages. . . . The Chinese cigar-makers. . . . [are] ruining the cause of white labor" (13, 121). Although the intensity of Schouler's investment in this position is parodied, his sentiments are later endorsed by the omniscient narrator, who, speaking of Trina's maidservant, comments that she is "miserably poor, her trade [laundry] long since ruined by Chinese competition" (194). As with other nativist texts, however, the concern with the repercussions of immigrant labor on native workers' wage levels is rapidly subordinated to Norris's chief preoccupation: immigrants' inadequate consumption habits and their effects within the larger socioeconomic context.

Fittingly, the novel opens with McTeague looking down on a Polk Street animated by the activities and fluctuating rhythms of consumption. From his dental parlors, McTeague has a vantage point on "corner drug stores with huge jars of red, yellow, and green liquids . . . restaurants, in whose windows one saw piles of unopened oysters weighted down by cubes of ice, and china pigs and cows knee deep in layers of white beans" (5). The regularly changing spectacle "never fail[s] to interest" McTeague, who gazes down on ladies engaged "at their morning's marketing. . . . [gathered around] boxes of berries and fruit" (5, 7). Later in the evening, provisions shops closed, he observes the engagement in leisure consumption: "There was [now] no thought but for amusement. The cable cars were loaded with theater-goers" (8). The scene is repeated at intervals throughout the text, and after her marriage Trina sits at this same vantage point: "As often as she raised her head she could see the big market, a confectionery store" (181). The ongoing and cyclical processes of consumption constitute both a backdrop against which the drama of McTeague and Trina is played out and the medium of that tragedy; for Norris, the market functions as a type of racial litmus test.

Within this setting, we are first introduced to McTeague, who is engaged in his regular, albeit primitive, consumption habits: "reading the paper, drinking his beer, and smoking . . . while his food digested; crop-full, stupid, and warm" (1). Within the context of an abundance economy, it is these habits that signal McTeague's civic potential rather than his fulfillment of his mother's Algeresque ambition to "have her son . . . rise in life and enter a profession" (2).

For Patten, unsophisticated, gluttonous consumption characterizes the worker, who, accustomed to an economy of scarcity, reacts under the new conditions of abundance to an overindulgence in sedative pleasures: "Rich ozone and the tang of winds once gave to the ancestors of the sedentary factory worker the zest in physical being for which immorality and intemperance are now mere counterfeits in the life of the city toiler. Drinking and the new sedative pleasures of smoking and saloon card-games are . . . an unintelligent attempt to enrich an impoverished, alien situation" (123). For that reason, Patten particularly approved of working-class entertainments such as "the melodramatic and exciting presentation of life processes in the people's theatres" (132). No matter how seemingly tawdry the entertainment, such leisure pursuits provide a stimulative effect that counters the laborer's tendency to torpid overindulgence. Although the worker's "perceptions are dull, his vision vague" (124), such intellectual lethargy can be counteracted: "The cheap magician of a vaudeville can excite the primitive curiosity of the mass and his claptrap thrill it into thought" (133). And that provocation to thought in the sphere of public leisure has ramifications for civic and national life generally, because people are thereby encouraged "to displace crude individual gratifications with grouped pleasures" (138). Once the induction into the latter begins, Patten argued that workers move beyond the desire to selfishly gratify individual pleasures and "turn eagerly to those [interests] that are social. . . . the germ of civic goodness takes root. . . . [as does the desire] to be known as a well-cared-for husband . . . a contributor to fraternal organizations" (141).

McTeague, in the early part of the novel, fulfills Patten's predictions about the effects of the market on primitive man as he becomes progressively civilized through his engagement in increasingly sophisticated acts of consumption. His efforts to court Trina include a visit to the theater, at which the "horseplay delighted McTeague beyond measure. He roared and shouted . . . slapping his knee, wagging his head" (100). The narrator's corrosive condescension at his characters' naive wonder at the entertainment's cheap spectacle ("art could go no farther" [101]) is mitigated by a Patten-like approval of what such leisure pursuits potentially presage. After his marriage, McTeague, now under the tutelage of Trina, begins to broaden the sphere of his interests and acquire more discrimination in his consumption: "Gradually the dentist improved . . . his little wife. . . . caused him to substitute bottled beer in the place of steam beer" (190). He begins to change his linen shirts once a week and demand clean cuffs daily; eventually, he purchases a silk hat. Together, the couple makes trips to art galleries and to the annual mechanic's fair, where they "study the exhibits carefully" (196). Such leisure consumption, observes the narrator in a paragraph that echoes Patten's arguments, leads McTeague to "observe the broader, larger interests of life, interests that affected him not as an individual, but as a member of a class, a profession, or a political party. . . . He commenced to have opinions, convictions—it was not fair to deprive tax-paying women of the privilege to vote . . . the Catholic priests were to be restrained in their efforts to gain control of the public schools" (191). McTeague's ambition for a house of his own, complete with six rooms and calla lilies, represents the apex of the transformation wrought by such progressive consumption.

Logically enough, McTeague's entrance into civic culture and the realm of political opinions entails the assumption of concern about the social effects of immigration, signaled in the preceding passage by his apprehensions about Catholic efforts to control public schools. Of course, the irony is that McTeague, although entertaining such notions about the socially destructive effect of immigration, is unable to recognize the far more insidious and immediately relevant threat posed by that phenomenon: the general lowering of living standards and retardant effect on that very market economy that has enabled his civic advance. Nor, of course, can he recognize that his wife, Trina, is the chief agent of that process in his immediate context.

It is Trina's accession to a fortune that, indirectly, pauperizes her husband. Marcus Schouler's jealousy over McTeague's good fortune in having become engaged to Trina before she wins the lottery incites him to inform city hall that his friend is an uncertified dentist. As a result, McTeague loses the ability to practice his profession. Schouler's jealousy, as well as McTeague's initial pleasure in Trina's newfound prosperity, stems partly from the expectation that McTeague, as her husband, will benefit from that wealth. For nativists, such naiveté was characteristic of the arguments of those who touted the economic benefits of immigration. They countered that immigrant enrichment would detract from, rather than augment, native citizens' financial well-being. McTeague's expectation of enrichment can only be maintained by ignoring Trina's assertion that "it's *mine*, every single penny of it. . . . Mine, mine" (155). It is Trina's growing reluctance to spend, however, that most definitively effects McTeague's social and economic demise. His progressive entertainment of various familial and civic ambitions is interrupted by his wife, when, faced with the possibility of renting a house complete with (dusty) calla lilies, she "tilt[s] back her heavy tiara of swarthy hair. . . . [and says] 'I don't think we can afford it'" (202).

Trina is one of a series of Norris's foreign female characters whose racial degeneracy, initially concealed, has a corrosive effect on the Anglo-Saxon males with whom they are involved. In his short story "After Strange Gods," initially grouped by Norris in a section of stories entitled "Outward and Visible Signs," narrative concern centers on the exposure of a foreign woman's latent racial depravity. The hero, Rouverey, one of Norris's many cardboard Anglo-Saxons (he has a "rugged . . . mind" [191] and "a big yellow beard" [192]), falls in love with Lalo Da, a beautiful Chinese woman. Unwisely, Rouveroy "simply took her for herself, as she was, without consideration, comment, or comparison" (191). Lalo Da eventually contracts smallpox, which reduces her face to "a grinning mask" (195). The disfigurement signals her true, racially degenerate nature, which is, as the narrator points out, "only half civilized . . . and . . . [that of] a woman" (195). Obtaining a poison that she transmits to him through a kiss, Lalo Da blinds Rouveroy so he can no longer see the "visible sign" (the pox), which represents her true, racial, nature. Thereafter, they live together quite happily, "the one distorted by disease and the other blind" (197).

Similar themes emerge in "A Case for Lombroso." Here, the principal characters are an Anglo-Saxon, Stayne, "just out of Harvard. . . . a 'torrowbred' to his very boots. . . . [and] liked because of his genuineness and his fine male strength" (35), and a Spanish woman, Cresencia Hromada, whose "hysterical sensitiveness" is due to the fact that her "race was almost exhausted . . . [and she was] a degenerate" (36). After Cresencia develops a passion for Stayne, her nature, hitherto characterized by "pride," becomes transformed into a "veritable fury. The red-hot, degenerate Spanish blood of her sang in her veins. . . . She used to sit in her room . . . rolling her head to and fro upon her folded arms, or biting at the bare flesh of them, in a very excess of passion" (38). Cresencia's sexual attraction transforms her from a woman with "superb, almost imperial, nonchalance" (38) to a "young girl of degenerate blood and jangled nerves and untamed passions" (39). She proceeds to entrap the former Harvardite in her sexual web and serves as the agent of his destruction. Both are ostracized by society, and the story ends with their mutual social ruin: "Stayne's name has long since been erased from the rolls of his club. Miss Hromada is thoroughly declassé. . . . Stayne goes to see her four nights in the week" (42).

Hromada's masochism recalls that of Trina. Too, the initial invisibility of Hromada's racial difference resembles that of the subsequent character. Although Hromada is of Spanish blood, she is "a rare one . . . [and] fair" (35). Trina's skin, too, is so fair that she appears almost anaemic, as if "all the vitality . . . had been sucked up into the strands and coils of [her] . . . hair" (161). Her racial degeneracy is all the more nefarious in that her physiognomy does not announce the degeneracies lurking within. Norris does hint early and repeatedly at these degeneracies, however, although McTeague proves unable to interpret the signs of racial difference. It is, of course, Trina's "marvelous black hair" that intimates her latent depravity. The narrator frequently lingers upon these "coils," remarking upon their "odorousness" and hue. His most frequent term for its color is *swarthy:* It is "a royal crown of swarthy bands" (23) and an "enormous tiara of swarthy hair" (258). Nativist animosity was particularly directed against what Clinton Stoddard Burr had dubbed the "swarthy white" races, and the narrator's early descriptions of Trina's hair clearly portend her later racial regression.

Before that, however, Trina's superlative ability as a financial manager is stressed. "Economy was her strong point," and "it soon became apparent that Trina would be an extraordinarily good housekeeper" (134). She makes successful "breathless . . . raids upon the bargain counters" (130) in which she purchases "'crêpe paper to make a lamp shade . . . a pair of Nottingham lace curtains for *forty-nine cents* . . . and some chenille portieres for two and a half'" (130, emphasis in the original). Her ability to furnish a comfortable home on a limited budget in these early months of her marriage recalls John Brandt's description of the Anglo-Saxon woman, who has "wonderful tact in arranging cozy-corners, dens"

(173). Trina's purchase of labor-intensive goods such as Nottingham lace marks her as hopelessly old-fashioned to those "candy store girls and florists' apprentices" (280) whose preference for mass-produced goods signals their modernity: "Whoever thinks of buying Nottingham lace now-a-days? Say, don't that *jar* you?" (280). Trina's commodity preferences and purchasing habits underscore the fact that she is a product of, and functions efficiently within, a producer economy; her frugality and thrift serve her well within that context.

The bestowal of $5,000 by the lottery system delivers Trina from an economy of scarcity into one of abundance. But the deliverance neither induces her to elevate her living standards nor incites her to consume more. On the contrary, her accession to wealth triggers a nascent parsimony that steadily increases in intensity as the novel unfolds. After she is "dowered by the company," her frugal ways perversely intensify, and her racial degeneracy flowers in a flagrant and morbid acquisitiveness: "In her fear lest their great good luck should . . . lead to habits of extravagance, she had recoiled too far in the other direction" (188). Norris underscores her parsimony again and again. Her "instinct of hoarding" emerges (202); every "instinct of her parsimony [becomes] aroused" (205); and "all her intuitive desire of saving, her instinct of hoarding, her love of money for the money's sake, rose strong within her" (209).

In a passage that recalls the arguments of Nathaniel Shaler, Norris explains the root of this parsimony: "A good deal of peasant blood still ran undiluted in her veins and she had all the instinct of a hardy and penurious mountain race—the instinct which saves without any thought, without any idea of consequence—saving for the sake of saving, hoarding without knowing why" (134). Her shift from frugality into miserliness under the impress of unexpected wealth signals the constitutional inability of the immigrant to function within the emergent market context. Her inability to recognize the inappropriateness of her old economic behavior in the face of changed financial circumstances is demonstrated in her repeated assertion that her frugality is a "good fault." "Never, never, never should a penny of that miraculous fortune be spent" (188) she vows. Circumstances have rendered her economic habits perverse: "Oftentimes when a considerable alleviation of . . . unhappiness could have been obtained at the expense of a nickel or a dime, Trina refused" (285). Small wonder then that her sexual practices incline increasingly toward the masochistic. Trina's sexual and consuming behaviors both derive from the logic that underpins an economy of scarcity in which pleasure is derived from painful habits of self-denial and from the suspension and withholding of gratification.

The gradual nature of Trina's regression serves Norris in a number of ways. Most important, it enables him to demonstrate his Patten-like faith in the civilizing power of the market while simultaneously voicing severe reservations about its power with respect to the immigrant. Before her racial degeneration, Trina's introduction of McTeague to a series of progressively more refined consumer and leisure pursuits bears out Patten's thesis about the efficacy of leisure consumption in inducting primitive people into modern civilization. For Norris, however, the market's acculturating efficacy is limited to native primitive types. Not only does Trina eventually and definitively regress to racial type upon acquiring wealth, but, as nativists had long warned, she also draws her husband down to a living standard whose squalor exceeds anything he previously countenanced. In the largest sense, too, one might argue that the hostility directed against Trina because of her inability to retrofit herself for an emergent consumer culture is in part a by-product of a conflict engendered in the native population by the larger cultural imperative to so retool oneself. The difficulties of trading in long-entrenched Victorian habits of thrift and conservation find expression in the narrative animosity accruing around Trina's refusal to do so.

Trina does not bank her ferociously guarded hoard within the mainstream financial system. Rather, she invests it in her uncle's toy manufacturing business. Uncle Oelberman is also an immigrant, hence Trina's pecuniary actions buttress the arguments of native commentators about immigrants' tendency to siphon money out of the mainstream fiscal infrastructure. In *Immigration and the Future*, for example, Frances Kellor chronicled the existence of what she termed the "racial economy"—a system of immigrant-owned banks, manufacturers, and merchants that immigrants tended to patronize exclusively and that kept immigrant funds circulating only within their communities. Eventually, however, Trina refuses to invest her money anywhere. She withdraws it from Oelberman's business, preferring to store it in a chamois bag in her bedroom. As she tumbles further and further back toward her racial roots, she also regresses with regard to financial acumen. As Kellor argued, "The native American [with their first wages in pocket] . . . thinks of how he can best have a good time; and if he saves any money, how it can be made to earn more money. [The immigrant]. . . . often stuffs [his savings] into his belt or under a mattress. The world of capital, investments, dividends, stocks and securities is unknown to him" (*Immigration and the Future* 199–200).

As Trina succumbs to her racial instincts, her destruction of her husband proceeds apace. Her miserly and slatternly proclivities take over, and she moves the protesting McTeague to progressively cheaper and more degraded quarters, despite the fact that she possesses a fortune. Initially they move to a one-room flat, which, although still on Polk Street, "looked down . . . upon the roofs of the hovels that bordered the alley" (271). Her refusal to heed McTeague's request to "take a little of your money an' . . . fix it up" is unlinked to any consideration other than the desire to save (273). As the narrator puts it, "It was not mere economy with her now. It was a panic terror lest a fraction of a cent of her savings should be touched; a passionate eagerness to continue to save. . . . Trina could have easily afforded better quarters" (274).

Her actions bear out the accusations of contemporary commentators such as U.S. Consul Jonas, who argued that immigrants "actually try to live . . . on a scale even more degraded than at home, in order to increase their savings" (Warne 173). The McTeagues' final domicile is a single room that "look[s] out into a grimy maze of back yards" (335). It is filled with "dirty unwashed crockery, greasy knives," and Trina's refusal to clean causes "cockroaches [to] appear. . . . All the filth of the alley invaded their quarters" (336–37). McTeague's vociferous objections to the continual lowering of their standards of living prove vain, and the luxury goods to which he has become accustomed are summarily withdrawn: "He had come to be very proud of his silk hat and 'Prince Albert' coat. . . . Trina had made him sell both. . . . He liked to wear clean cuffs; Trina allowed him a fresh pair on Sundays only" (285–86). Eventually, after a period of struggle to maintain his standards, "all of a sudden, he slipped back" (286), his fate resonating with nativist warnings that the low standard of living of the incoming races would inevitably drag down the standards of native workers and families.

Trina's parsimony eventually causes her brutalized husband to steal money from her and desert her. His loss of profession, social position, and home are all effects of his interaction with her. His daily occupation now consists of "fishing. . . . At noon he would retire to a bit of level turf . . . and cook his fish . . . eating them without . . . knife or fork" (333). He has joined the ranks of those "self-respecting [native] men" who, under the impress of immigration, have been turned "into day laborers, odd job men . . . and 'hoboes'" (Ross 208–9). After McTeague has "spent her money . . . in royal fashion" (364), he returns to steal more. Trina's resistance induces him to bludgeon her to death. The brutal murder—the climax of the novel—constitutes, in the context of nativists' economic arguments, a blow for the native worker against the "swarthy white," whose frugality emerges as a national threat in the context of a market economy.

The recurrence of the figure of immigrant woman within the nativists' economic discourse continued well into the second decade of the twentieth century. Therefore, it is entirely apposite that Frank Warne concluded his popularizing update of Mayo-Smith's theories in 1913 with a description of a desk ornament that had an unnerving trompe l'oeil effect: It "represented the nude figure of a woman so posed as to form an exact life-like reproduction of a grinning skull" (*Immigrant Invasion* 278). The effect, argued Warne, was analogous to that created by the issue of immigration. Those who cleaved to sentimental notions concerning America's status as refuge of the oppressed were unable to see the "skull" (the economically deleterious effects of the inrushing horde). Those concerned with economic issues, however, "do not see that view which is typified in the graceful figure of the beautiful woman of the desk ornament. Instead, conspicuous to them is the grinning skull" (279). The phantasmatic figure of the immigrant woman recurred in Warne's text as in the narratives of all those nativists who attend to the economic effects of immigration. It embodied the linked economic and cultural ills flowing from the massed national presence of individuals irredeemably immersed in premodern economic practices.

4

Sentimental Ambitions: Americanization and the "Isolated and Alien" Mother

> But surely there is another scene of colonial discourse in which
> the native or Negro meets the demand of colonial discourse. . . .
> The colonial fantasy. . . . proposes a teleology—under certain
> conditions of colonial domination and control the native
> is progressively reformable.
>
> —Homi K. Bhabha

> Can we permit thousands of foreign mothers to hold their old
> country ideals unchanged and expect their homes to be truly
> American? . . . We must bring the mother out of her home. . . .
> When we can do that we shall save families from disruption,
> for the mother determines the home; we shall save America,
> for the home determines America.
>
> —Bessie Olga Pehotsky

DESPITE NATIVIST assertions to the contrary, a number of writers and reformers proclaimed the immigrants' potential for rehabilitation and directed their energies toward achieving that task. The momentum of this project, known as the Americanization movement, peaked during and in the years immediately following America's participation in World War I. Its inception can be traced to the early 1890s and located specifically in the work of the social settlements, in the various programs launched by the Daughters of the American Revolution to educate immigrants in American customs, and in the work of individual activists such as Jacob Riis (Higham, *Strangers* 236–37).[1]

Buttressed by the accounts of scientists such as Franz Boas (whose report for the Dillingham Commission asserted that modification of immigrants' living conditions and nutritional habits led to a definitive change in the racial constitution of their descendants), Americanizers proclaimed that the aliens could jettison their Old World cultures.[2] They perceived the immigrant to be eminently malleable. Their difference no longer sprang from a genetic and inalienable source but was susceptible to modification. Key tactics in this collective effort at racial renovation included forays into tenements to gather information (the photographic missions of Jacob Riis), attempts to recolonize the "wilderness" (the settlement movement), and direct visitation of immigrant homes in order to teach American ways by example.[3]

The immigrant mother was a particular target of these reformers' correctional zeal.[4] In 1920 Kate Waller Barrett, a special agent for the U.S. Immigration Service, summarized the prodigious effort required of native Americans if the ever-burgeoning immigrant population were to be successfully assimilated. She pinpointed the immigrant family home as the critical site for the native's assimilationist endeavors and reiterated an imperative at least three decades old: "The importance of reaching the alien woman is paramount if we are going to Americanize our foreign population" (224). Continuing, she asserted that the immigrant mother was "the crux of the whole subject" (224). Frances Kellor, chief of New York State's Bureau of Industries and Immigration, agreed, arguing that "the foreign-born woman and her home are . . . the most vulnerable spots in our . . . democracy" ("Neighborhood Americanization" 9).[5] Peter Speek, a contributor to the Carnegie Series on Americanization Studies, articulated the opinion of the bulk of these reformers when he argued, "Whether immigrant women vote or not, they are an inevitable influence in the political life of the country. . . . The first question is how to reach them" (227).

Part of the reason the immigrant mother and home were particular targets of concern is that they were seen to fall outside the network of institutions (public schools, factories, and prisons) in which the inculcation of American ideals might otherwise occur. Kellor explained, "The foreign born child is Americanized by the public school. . . . Men become Americanized at work," but the mother still wears "a shawl over her head" ("Neighborhood Americanization" 9, 10). Americanizers (in the face of abundant evidence to the contrary) conceived the immigrant woman to be isolated within the tenement and stressed the need to penetrate into that region in order to bring her within the ambit of Americanization.[6] More important, it was these activists' conception of the role of the mother in the reproduction of racial difference that positioned her at the forefront of their campaign.[7] This conception, in turn, owed to the convergence of cultural racist presuppositions and sentimental ideology within the activists' racial schema.

Cultural racists typically see the home as the critical space for the transmission of racial difference: "The family. . . . is portrayed as the crucial site for the reproduction of those correct social mores, attitudes and behaviours that are thought to be essential to maintaining a 'civilized' society" (Lawrence, "Just Plain Common Sense" 50).[8] Accordingly, Americanizers pinpointed the immigrant home as a key location for implementing their normative coercion and positioned it, in their cultural-racist terms, as the place in which a retrogressive culture would issue in a dysfunctional family. The logic informing this project was thoroughly sentimental. The immense popularity that sentimental novels had enjoyed during the middle decades of the nineteenth century had largely waned by the early 1900s.[9] As Laura Wexler has demonstrated, however, that fictional genre's political agenda came to inform several reform movements during the Progressive Era.[10] Sentimental novels typically stage the desire of marginalized characters such as slaves or working-class children to replicate white, middle-class codes of conduct. By remaking themselves in the image of the dominant culture, such individuals prove their eligibility for normative citizenship.[11] In other words, sentimental fiction contains an assimilationist vision at its core.

Wexler maintains that Progressive programs designed to Americanize immigrants (along with educational efforts aimed at native American and African-American populations) coupled the imperial agenda of sentimental fiction with "the social control of marginal domestic populations" (18). The Americanization movement implemented the reform agenda of sentimental fiction within a variety of institutional settings, both in its conviction of the other's mutability and in the modes by which it proposed to effect that transformation (namely, through the media of instruction and affective connection). The political program underpinning Jacob Riis's documentary chronicle of immigrant life in the slums or Sophinisba Breckinridge's sociological analysis of the immigrant woman's assimilatory potential in *New Homes for Old* was, therefore, directly linked to the fiction of such mid-century writers as Maria Cummins, Harriet Beecher Stowe, and Susan Warner.[12]

The Americanizers' focus on the immigrant mother and their forms of representing her are equally indebted to sentimental ideology. The power afforded therein to the woman within the home, the idea that "the mother is the greatest educator of the nation" (Speek 227), rendered the alien woman critical to the success of their movement. Her formative influence on the next generation made her racial reconstruction imperative if immigrants were to be reshaped into American citizens. The success of the assimilationist efforts of those home nurses, settlement house workers, and social workers who ventured into tenements to teach the necessity for, and pragmatics of, accomplishing rapid and thorough Americanization largely depended upon the immigrant mother's acquiescence to these regulatory interventions. Margaret Sangster, drawing from the sentimental credo, warned, "The tenement mother, whatever her creed, or race, or country, impresses herself upon her family with an ineffaceable stamp" (242). "Reaching the immigrant woman" became the critical component of the reformers' campaign. Their task was to impart those practices and skills that would enable the immigrant woman to carry out her sentimental maternal role.

Of course, this was more than a little ironic because such a position was not an option for the vast majority of immigrant women. Evelyn Nakao Glenn has pointed out that the "idealized division of labor" upon which the ideology of sentimental motherhood depended "was largely illusory for . . . immigrant and racial-ethnic families" (4).[13] To the degree that the immigrant woman engaged in activities calculated to aid her family in negotiating the economic conditions of the new world (home-work, taking in boarders, and putting her children to work as early as possible), she violated the precepts of normative maternity. To the extent that she herself engaged in waged labor, she moved outside of the intensely privatized world of the home to which the True Mother was confined and upon which depended her claim to normative citizenship. Americanizers elided these economic exigencies, however. Instead, they presented inadequate training combined with retrograde cultural practices as the factors militating against the alien woman's achievement of the ideal. Successful Americanization depended largely on an innate capacity and willingness to absorb those New World mothering practices modeled by social workers.

The Americanizers' immersion in sentimental "ways of seeing" produced a thorough ambivalence in their representations of the immigrant mother.[14] Whereas nativists had posited an antithetical relationship between the immigrant woman and sentimental maternity, Americanizers stressed her aspirations toward that ideal and read those aspirations as testament to her desire to assimilate. Her circumstantial inability to approximate that ideal (given that her culture and education left her inadequate to its demands) rendered the alien mother a figure of particular pathos for these activists. Their texts frequently depicted her as a suffering Madonna in order to convey that pathos. The premier journal of social work, *The Survey*, typically construed the immigrant mother in this way. The cover of the April 5, 1913, issue carried an illustration of a sculpture of "The Immigrant Mother" by Antoinette B. Hollister. Hollister's image was also reproduced inside the December 6, 1913, issue, this time accompanied by verses on the same theme by Madelaine Sweeny Miller and Gordon Thayer. In the October 11, 1913, issue, a sketch of "A Bohemian Immigrant Mother" by E. Benedict of Hull House appeared, and the December 11, 1915, issue contained a reproduction of a postcard produced for the National Child Labor Committee and entitled "The Immigrant Madonna," with verses on the same topic by Helen C. Dwight. Even after the cessation of the war and the curtailing of foreign immigration, the December 1, 1922, issue carried an illustration of "The Immigrant Madonna" from a monotype by Joseph Stella (fig. 1). As Stephanie Smith explains, "Sanctified maternity [had] become . . . a central image for the nineteenth-century white, middle-class Cult of True Womanhood" (75).[15] Americanizers drew repeatedly upon that familiar icon in the first two decades of the twentieth century. The suffering alien woman whose maternal effectivity could be restored by native intervention proved a powerful sign of the necessity as well as the tenability of their project.

Notwithstanding their investment in conveying the immigrant woman's sentimental ambitions, Americanizers' narratives were invariably shadowed by accounts of her refractoriness with respect to their pedagogical efforts. For example, "Old Country Mothers and American Daughters," Christina Merriman's review of Louise Montgomery's *The American Girl in the Stockyards,* was accompanied in *The Survey* by a photograph of immigrant women clad in head scarves and

FIGURE 1. "The Immigrant Madonna," from a monotype by Joseph Stella. (Library of Congress)

shawls. The photograph appears taken from a considerable distance, and the women seem to be hurrying out of the camera's field of vision. "Immigrant Mothers, Immune to American Influences" runs the rather ominous caption. The women's distance from and apparent ignorance of the camera bespeak that immunity, as does their stubbornly traditional garb. The image taps into what by 1913 was a familiar narrative about the immigrant mother's particular imperviousness to instruction. In fact, the narrative was so commonplace that the writer felt no need to explain or expound upon it and left the photograph and caption to speak for themselves. Neither in the accompanying review nor across the range of Americanizers' texts, however, is the immigrant woman's recalcitrance presented as a consequence of her active resistance to Americanization. Rather, her perceived inability to retrofit herself is also a product of her construal within the terms of sentimental discourse. Ultimately, these reformers' construction of the immigrant woman as a sentimental mother immobilized her with respect to the process of assimilation. The discourse of Americanization ultimately joined with that of nativism in reifying the immigrant mother as constitutionally unassimilable.[16]

Jacob Riis's texts provide an early and comprehensive treatment of the "immigrant problem" from an Americanizer's perspective. A police reporter turned agitator for tenement-house reform, Riis was concerned to speed assimilation through the improvement of the immigrants' environment, and he conducted several fact-gathering expeditions into New York's tenements in order to record and report the conditions that obtained there. His books detailing the need for reform within the tenements—*How the Other Half Lives* (1890), *The Battle with the Slum* (1901), and *The Peril and the Preservation of the Home* (1903), among many others—were the first on this topic to reach a large audience. They largely consist of photographs embedded within a written narrative, a novel format that was especially effective in the case of *How the Other Half Lives,* which went through eleven editions in five years (Szasz and Bogardus 422).

The use of photography augmented the "authenticity" of Riis's representations (Szasz and Bogardus 429). Sally Stein has demonstrated, however, that despite the use of new photographic and reproductive technologies his work was firmly located in the "literary tradition of the urban picturesque" that characteristically mixed sketches and narrative exposés of the seamy underworld of city life (10). Despite the fact that the photographs' effectiveness depended on the willingness of his contemporaries to extend to the photographic apparatus the capacity to reproduce the "truth," Maren Stange has shown that his images were far from being unmediated reproductions of a spontaneous reality. Rather, Riis composed

the tableaux in his snapshots, sometimes paying subjects to pose in certain attitudes and often cropping both his own prints and those he borrowed from other
photographers in order to achieve a more satisfactory effect (Stange 7).[17] In the
case of "Bandit's Roost," a photograph taken by Richard Hoe Lawrence but included in the Riis Collection at the Museum of the City of New York, Stange has
shown how Riis cropped the photograph horizontally in order to excise two
women from the tableau. The image, which reveals a tenement alley crowded with
men, some of whom wield sticks, is thereby rendered considerably more threatening (Stange 7–9). Such techniques, although undeniably detracting from the
images' documentary status, are congruent with Riis's conception of the nature
of his photographic practice. As Stange argues, Riis conceived his work to be
closer to art than to objective journalism. He "uses the metaphors of art to em-
bellish his text" and "specifically associates photography with the traditionally
sanctioned 'magical' powers of art and poetry rather than with innovation and
social insight" (25–26).

Riis's reworking of the nativist image of the immigrant mother was fundamental to the rhetorical power of his lectures and texts. That reworking was extremely
influential. In *Battle with the Slum* he maintained that "there is nothing better
in all the world" than "the mother heart" (251) and defined his task as reformer
to be the institution of a normative family life among the immigrants, a task vital
to the well-being of the state: "Unsafest of all is any thing or deed that strikes at
the home, for from the people's home proceeds citizen virtue, and nowhere else
does it live" (7).

For Riis, the home was always metonymically connected with the mother. His
reform efforts, directed toward the immediate goal of eliminating overcrowded
tenement conditions (in other words, rectifying a situation in which homes were
without mothers and mothers without homes), were largely an attempt to institute the conditions in which a normative motherhood could operate. According to the dictates of sentimentality, however, Riis's immigrant mother had to
emerge as sorely inadequate, because it was the perceived breakdown of the
maternal bond in the tenement that legitimated his intervention. The lack of fit
between the idealized mother and immigrant reality was a gap into which Riis,
and by extension his native readers, would have to step.

The rhetorical appeal of the photograph entitled "In the Home of an Italian
Ragpicker, Jersey Street" (fig. 2) is largely a result of its depiction of the foreign
woman as an aspirant sentimental mother.[18] As with many of Riis's photographs
involving immigrant women, the intimacy of context (the viewer penetrates into
the inner recesses of immigrant family life) is striking. Riis's use of the novel
technology of flash photography allowed him to photograph domestic spaces that
middle-class readers had hitherto only imagined.[19] The passivity of the mater-

nal figure, however, here delivering herself up to the controlling gaze of Riis's lens, allays anxieties potentially attendant upon this unprecedented proximity. The effectiveness of the image turns on what John Tagg has called "a social division between the power and privilege of *producing* and *possessing* meaning and the burden of *being* meaning" (6, emphasis in the original).[20] The utter acquiescence of the woman to Riis's disciplinary surveillance is key to Riis's argument about her assimilatory potential. The willingness with which she yields herself to the camera bespeaks her susceptibility to being remolded in the American context, would Americans only intervene to facilitate it.

Riis's mother and child are posed in a conventional Madonna and child tableau, the mother centered, seated, and holding her young baby in her arms. Yet it is the depiction's deviations from, as much as correspondences to, the familiar representation that compel attention. The Italian mother's gaze is not cast at her baby; she does not return the baby's look but instead directs her gaze above the camera level. Although the traditional iconography of the Madonna often

FIGURE 2. "In the Home of an Italian Ragpicker, Jersey Street." (The Jacob A. Riis Collection no. 157, Museum of the City of New York)

depicts her with eyes cast upward as a sign of submission, within this context the interplay of looks not only conveys the notion of supplication but also, combined with the mother's physical posture, reinforces the separation of the mother and child. Rather than bending protectively over it, she seems split from the baby, defying the usual monadic image that the tableau of Madonna and child offers. Nancy Theriot has pointed out that a critical part of the nineteenth-century "mother-script" assumed a total commitment on the part of mothers toward their children, a commitment that "involved physical and attitudinal expectations that bound mothers spatially, behaviorally, and emotionally to their children's welfare" (27).[21] Thus, the physical separation between Riis's mother and child stresses their emotional separation. The mother's body is not surrendered to the baby (Theriot 27). Instead, in direct contrast to the devotion that Riis had elsewhere declared as vital—"every baby is entitled to one pair of mother's arms around its neck; that is its God-given right" (*Peril* 23)—the mother mechanically clasps the child as if it were a bundle to be held rather than something to be nurtured. Once again, its rigid form emphasizes its spatial and emotional separation from the mother. The rolled-up mattresses stacked on barrels and the grimy buckets that surround the Italian woman attest to the circumstantial conditions that contribute to her maternal inadequacies.

Then, too, the fact that the baby is swaddled points to the existence of archaic and outmoded mothering practices that demand modernization and the intercession of the reformer. Breckinridge argued that because immigrant parents came from "countries . . . which . . . are not republics," they tended to insist, in un-American fashion, on "the absolute obedience of child to parent" (152).[22] That relationship was antithetical to democratic participation because only "early placing of the responsibility for his acts on the child himself" would "train citizens for . . . democracy" (151). The child's swaddling is part of the narrative's argument about this immigrant mother's ignorance of American child-rearing practices and her consequent inability to fulfill her nationally significant maternal role.

Lillian Wald's *The House on Henry Street* (1915) also employed a rhetoric of deficient maternity that simultaneously underscored the conflict between the woman's desire to fulfill the ideal of sentimental motherhood and her inability to do so.[23] It details an encounter between Wald and an Italian mother: "Once in searching for a patient in a large tenement near the Bowery I knocked at each door in turn. An Italian woman hesitatingly opened one, no wider than to give me a glimpse of a slight creature obviously stricken with fear. Her face brought instantly to my mind the famous picture of the sorrowing mother. 'Dolorosa!' I said. The tone and the word sufficed, and she opened the door. . . . In a corner of the room lay two children with marks of starvation upon them" (286–87).

Wald's relation to the immigrant is shown to be an aestheticized one before her textualization of the event: "Her face brought instantly to my mind *the famous picture of* the sorrowing mother" (emphasis added). Inherent maternal sentiment provides a shared language that is assumed to transcend cultural and ethnic barriers ("Dolorosa! I said . . . she opened the door"). Equally important, the immigrant woman's failure to approximate the maternal ideal calls for Wald's intervention. She subsequently fetched food for the children and obtained the release of the woman's husband, who had been wrongfully imprisoned.[24] The passage is a striking example of how the rhetoric of sentimental motherhood can be mobilized both to legitimate native intervention into immigrants' lives and mount an argument for their potential recuperability for the American way of life.

As the new century unfolded, the definition of deficient maternity shifted as mothering became reformulated on a scientific basis and the acquisition of specific knowledge and skills became necessary. Correspondingly, the imperative to intervene into the immigrant mother's life became all the more urgent. Breckinridge now insisted that it was not merely an unwholesome environment that prevented immigrant women from carrying out their maternal duties, because "looking after the physical well-being of the children is. . . . a peculiarly difficult problem for the foreign-born mothers. Modern knowledge of child-feeding and modern ideas with regard to daily bathing are of recent origin" (150–51). Kellor likewise urged the appointment of home teachers who would visit immigrant homes, and she repeatedly underscored the necessity to impart to immigrant mothers information concerning the "use and preparation of American foods, care of children and homes" ("Neighborhood Americanization" 11).[25] The narratives of these later Americanizers are striking because activists, rather than replace the old rhetoric of sentiment with the new ideas of science, generally articulated that rhetoric with the emergent, scientific conception of maternity.

The photograph by Jessie Tarbox Beals that accompanied Dan Feeks's "Putting Mother in Her Right Place" (fig. 3) in *World Outlook* (1918) encapsulated the shift to the scientific ideal of motherhood while rearticulating elements from both the discourse of sentiment and the traditional iconography of the Madonna. A product of native intervention (Feeks recommended home education of immigrant mothers by social workers), the immigrant mother is dressed in spotless medical white. The baby's unencumbered body, free of swaddling, attests to freedom from archaic and handicapping mothering practices. The infant is alert, sitting up and gazing at something out of the photograph's frame, testament to a nascent individualism presaging the emergence of a fit democratic subject. At the same time, the circular form of the photograph, which contains nothing besides the pair, emphasizes their unity and invokes the familiar tableau of Madonna and child. The emotional bond between the two is evoked by the immi-

FIGURE 3. A successfully Americanized mother and her infant by Jessie
Tarbox Beals. (Library of Congress)

grant mother's gaze, which is directed at her baby, as well as by her attitude of
protective support. Here, science, imparted by the social worker, enables the
procession of the sentimental ideal, which in turn retrofits the immigrant as a
normative subject-citizen.

Riis's texts, predating this shift to science, largely content themselves with ges-
turing to the break-down of the requisite emotional bonds in the tenement. The
photograph "Organized Charity: A Home Nurse" (fig. 4) continues to deploy the
traditional iconography of mother and child but reverses it. The young boy rather
than the mother is the nurturer. While the "mother script," in which Riis's readers
were well schooled, called for a "commitment of body and soul to the service of
the offspring. . . . [in which the] mother was to be constantly available, constantly
selfless," in this photograph the impossibility of such commitments in the tenement is heavily underscored (Theriot 27). Once again, the mother does not return the gaze of her child. Represented as an inert, defeminized lump, she stares
out past him at something out of the picture's frame. The angle from which the

photograph is taken, as well as the cropping that cuts off the top of the pictures hanging on the wall, reduces the apparent size of the room. The futility of the attempt to institute a domesticity modeled on middle-class patterns, evidenced in markers such as the china cup, framed prints, intricately carved wooden door behind the mother's bed, and elaborately patterned quilt, is ironically under-

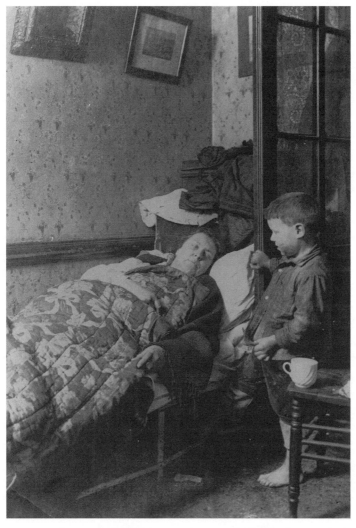

FIGURE 4. "Organized Charity: A Home Nurse." (The Jacob A. Riis Collection no. 18[?], Museum of the City of New York)

scored by the little boy's grime, loose shirt, and bare feet and, of course, by the prone mother. Yet those very markers, absent in Stephen Crane's depiction of Mrs. Johnson's domicile, witness the assimilatory potential of this malfunctioning family and urge the need for American intervention to facilitate it.

Reformers invariably hedged descriptions of immigrant women with doubts concerning her capacity to attain the ideal to which she aspired. In some cases she appeared stubbornly resistant to their instructional projects. Dan Feeks's shrill insistence that the "immigrant Mother. . . . must get . . . out of herself, out of a rut, out of her too-foreign habits" (9) insinuated a woman disturbingly unresponsive to reformers' agendas. What remained implicit in Feeks became explicit in the texts of many others. Again and again, reformers' texts described scenes of conflict between the immigrant mother and the native reformer, often enacted over the site of children. Joseph Mayper, writing of the resistance social workers encountered from immigrant women, explained that "great difficulty was experienced in this healthwork in overcoming the superstitions of ignorant mothers" (57). Consequently, "A decidedly threatening attitude had to be assumed by the nurse in several cases to convince the mothers of their folly" (57). The immigrant mother's dogged clinging to Old World ways was seen to lessen her control over children and husband, forcing a rupture in the family that led to the much-discussed criminal tendencies of the second generation of immigrant youth. In the face of the alien woman's "prefer[ence for] her own foods and ways" ("Neighborhood Americanization" 12) and tendency to become "suspicious and resentful and sullen" (17) in the face of Americanization efforts, Frances Kellor exhorted listeners at the Colony Club to "show them [immigrants] the advantages of the American standards and *insist* on their prevalence" (12, emphasis added).

In Elsa Herzfeld's 1905 account of her social work among immigrant women, a discussion of the foreign woman's ignorance of normative child-care practices slides, almost imperceptibly, into condemnation of her refusal to implement them. Herzfeld at first attributed the immigrant mother's inability to provide appropriate care for her children to ignorance: "The cultural status of many a tenement-house dweller is not far removed from that of primitive man. His world is a world of ghosts and spirits, of the reality of dreams and the efficacy of the amulet" (983). In the face of such "primitivism," it was essential for natives to school immigrants in the new technical expertise of domesticity. Herzfeld also acknowledged poverty as a factor influencing the procession of child care in tenements: "Children are not warmly wrapped. They have little underclothing. . . . The poor physical condition of the older children I attribute to the lack of suitable dietary" (986). Although poor mothering practices here derive from poverty ("little underclothing") and ignorance ("lack of a suitable dietary"), a subtle modulation in the paragraph shifts the blame onto the foreign mother's turpitude: "Sometimes the young child goes to school without breakfast because the mother is not up on time" (986). Again, although Herzfeld pointed out the need to educate the women—"most families are entirely ignorant of the precautions necessary to preserve the purity of milk" (986)—she went on to stress the foreign woman's resistance to advice: "[Although] they were glad to be taught how to pasteurize or sterilize the milk for baby . . . it 'took up too much time to do it regularly'" (986).[26]

For most of these writers, however, the immigrant mother's resistance was depicted as the result of apathy or incapacitation rather than as an active refusal to change. Isabelle Horton, superintendent of social and educational work in Chicago's Halsted Street Institutional Church, summarized the reformers' general perspective when she wondered, "How can these indifferent, these ignorant, these discouraged mothers be stimulated, taught, inspired?" (100). That imputed incapacitation is a critical part of the texts' rhetorical appeal. Riis's "In the Home of an Italian Ragpicker" clearly constructs the immigrant mother in this way, and the mother's literal prostration in "Organized Charity: A Home Nurse" surely gestures to a more generalized paralysis on her part in the face of New World demands. In *How the Other Half Lives,* Riis carefully recorded the contents of a note found with a baby abandoned in front of the Foundling Asylum and thereby staged the immigrant mother's admission of ineptitude. "'Take Care of Johnny, for God's Sake. I cannot,'" the note, penned "in a woman's trembling hand," read (145).

Later Americanizers, including Wald, Kellor, and Breckinridge, similarly defined the immigrant mother in terms of a generalized and intractable debility. Wald wrote that immigrant mothers are "not indifferent, but rather helpless, in the face of the modern city's demands upon motherhood" (198). Kellor particularly harped on that theme, arguing that the first step in the Americanization process was showing the immigrant woman "friendliness," because only that would enable her to "do her own thinking and changing . . . we [need to] . . . help create in her the *desire* for it" ("Neighborhood Americanization" 17). One typical description in Katherine Anthony's volume of case histories of working immigrant mothers concerns a Mrs. Furhmann, in whom "patience rather than enterprise is the chief trait" (179). The opening to Anthony's text asserts that "the mother of the family . . . least often sees beyond the neighborhood limits. . . . [is] even less adventurous in seeking recreation" (6–7). Acknowledging that these people "once had the enterprise to journey from the old world to the new" (11), she then proves that, as far as women are concerned, "Somehow they have lost it on the West Side" (11).

Breckinridge's *New Homes for Old* also cataloged the many difficulties facing the immigrant wife and mother in her new context. Subject to the tyrannical

dictates of her husband, in conflict with her children whose rapid Americanization pries them free of her control, and unschooled in the "art of spending," she
becomes "uncertain of herself" (175). For Breckinridge, the prototypical immigrant woman was "a Ukrainian mother, who admits being afraid to go beyond
her own neighborhood" (123–24). The text represents the immigrant woman as
an isolated and alien unit whose cultural stasis estranges her children. Breckinridge cited daughters who "said [they] were ashamed to go out with their mother
who remained unprogressive. . . . [who] would do nothing but sit at home and
cry" (184).

No doubt many immigrant women did find it difficult to adjust to new conditions. Yet the uniformity of this characterization of a hapless and refractory
immigrant mother, as well as the narrative energy invested in the depiction, owes
more to the reformers' immersion in a sentimental regime of intelligibility, combined with their need to legitimate their own activities, than to any anterior reality.[27] Depictions of immigrant mothers unable to fulfill their maternal functions constructed a domain for the authoritive expertise of the newly developed
profession of social work. Ellen Fitzpatrick and many other critics have shown
how closely the individual careers of professional women such as Breckenridge,
Kellor, and Wald were linked to the figure of the immigrant woman. Wald became nationally known as a settlement-house worker; Breckinridge's reputation
was secured, despite her academic position at the University of Chicago, as a social
worker among immigrants (Fitzpatrick 190); and Kellor's various government
positions were a function of her expertise on the issues of immigration and
Americanization. The recurrence of the incapable immigrant mother within their
texts can be traced, in part, to their own need to forge an acceptable professional
role for themselves, as women, in a society still committed to the ideology of dual
spheres. Positioning themselves as the necessary adjunct to the dysfunctional
immigrant family, these women assumed the role of public mothers (Smith-
Rosenberg 264). Their professional competence was secured against the backdrop of the inefficient immigrant mother.[28] And Sally Stein and Maren Stange
have shown that Jacob Riis, in exposing to the middle-class public the neediness
and threat of the immigrants and presenting himself as capable of mitigating that
neediness, forged a prominent social and public position for himself.[29]

It is important to note, however, that this conception of alien women as almost imbecilic in their inability to adapt to a changed milieu is also a function
of the reformers' immersion in sentimental "ways of seeing." Although demon-
strating her assimilatory ambitions, the alien mother's proto-sentimental construction immobilized her with respect to the process of Americanization. A brief
look at the gendered assumptions underlying sentimentalism demonstrates why.
Sentimental discourse assigned women to the domestic sphere, where they were

"charged with preserving old values and a safe and stable haven against change" (Evans 69). The literal and symbolic function of preserving the nation's traditions and cultural mores was a natural adjunct to her innate (biologically based) conservatism. Nineteenth- and early-twentieth-century biology assumed that "woman was in evolutionary terms 'the conservative element' to the man's 'progressive'" (Stepans 40). As Nearing and Nearing rehearsed this biological wisdom, "Since women are less specialized they are more conservative. That is, they have more of a tendency to adhere to the past, and less inclination to branch out in new directions" (16). Thus, the female "conserv[es] the qualities which have been developed and handed down from the past" (17). For reformers, the female sex's biologically mandated conservatism made the immigrant woman a particular point of concern because, unlike her male counterpart, it rendered her innately resistant to their instructional project. In order to assimilate, she would have to throw off her sex-determined conservatism and renege on her biological function of repository and transmitter of her own culture's mores.

Thus, the urgency impelling Kellor's assertion that "immigrant women are very generally years behind the men in Americanization" ("Straight America" 24) was largely an outcome of the projection of the sentimental ideal onto the immigrant female. Although her sentimentalized construal demonstrated a desire for cultural citizenship, it simultaneously implied assumptions about her innate aversion to change.[30] In other words, the sentimentalized immigrant woman was constitutionally at odds with the Americanizer's project; within the logic of sentimentality, the phrase "Americanized immigrant mother" is oxymoronic. Consequently, reformers' texts oscillated between reclaiming the immigrant woman for national belonging by depicting those factors that mitigated against the procession of her maternal duties and evincing a more or less muted animus against the alien female, who was, given the reformers' immersion within the gendered assumptions of sentimentality, biologically resistant to reformation.

Nowhere is evidence of the Americanizers' investment in biologically based explanations of gender difference more abundant than in the texts of those writers and activists who continued to stress the immigrant woman's dependence and conservatism even though clearly confronted with activities on her part that demonstrated enterprise and flexibility. Anthony's *Mothers Who Must Earn,* a fascinating and highly readable account of the experiences of laboring immigrant mothers on New York's West Side, is one such narrative. It combines descriptions of the work engaged in by the women, statistics pertaining to rates of pay and hours of work, and interviews with working immigrant mothers. Most pertinent to my argument is Anthony's dogged cleavage to the script of immigrant mothers as anachronistic, tradition-bound, and dependent despite being confronted time and again with evidence confirming their adaptability and survival skills.

She insisted that immigrant mothers who worked did so out of maternal considerations only: "They had become wage-earners in obedience to the most primitive of maternal instincts. Their children would have suffered seriously had they failed or refused to earn" (199; see also fig. 5). Anthony reclaimed the laboring immigrant mother for sentimental motherhood by defining her as doubly dependent. Contrasting the father's and children's job-seeking with that of the mother, she wrote: "Looking for work. . . . has for the boy or girl the spice of adventure. . . . But the mother who must earn finds it no adventure" (84). She continued, "A more helpless figure than the middle-aged mother of a family starting out to look for work would be hard to imagine" (85). A scant few pages later, however, she pointed out that "the women feel a strong mutual responsibility to help one another to find employment. . . . they roughly co-operate to help each other in work. . . . news of a vacant job is quickly passed around" (88–89). This clear conveyance of communal cooperation in the matter of employment opportunities surely bears witness to the women's enterprise. Anthony acknowledged the cooperation only to quickly subordinate it to the overriding agenda of the text: the reproduction of the immigrant woman as a sentimental mother and hence as hapless and inflexible (fig. 6).

FIGURE 5. "A Slavic Mother and Her Five Reasons for Working," from Katherine Anthony, *Mothers Who Must Earn*. (Library of Congress)

FIGURE 6. "A Victim of the Long Day. After the day's work in the laundry the mother must work all evening at home," from Katherine Anthony, *Mothers Who Must Earn*. (Library of Congress)

Again, discussing the large number of immigrant mothers who become janitresses, a much-coveted job, Anthony observed, "Occasionally, a janitress will develop very fair business capacity for her work. A large real estate dealer in the district says that he depends on the character of his janitresses to keep his apartments rented" (75). Yet Anthony continued to maintain that the women experienced a "complete stultification of spirit" from their "life of monotonous toil" (100). At one point, however, she edged very close to acknowledging that work, rather than being solely waged labor and an arena of travail, for many immigrant mothers provided a forum in which a welcome sociality could occur: "None of the women expressed a direct preference for outside work over housework. . . . some expressed a preference for cleaning jobs because of their social character. 'The work is hard,' said one, 'but we all pull together'" (158). Despite such evidence of resourcefulness and affirmation of paid labor, Anthony maintained that the immigrant mother's innate passivity and conservatism rendered her doubly disadvantaged. The tension between adaptive reality and sentimental template indicate that the Americanizers' sentimentalized understanding of the immigrant mother precluded recognition of her competence in the New World and in turn rendered her a well-nigh intractable problem in terms of their rehabilitatory project.

The convergence of nativist and Americanization arguments with respect to the immigrant woman's racial intransigence helps explain the periodic eruption into reformers' texts of maternal images at odds in every respect with the image of sanctified immigrant motherhood. Any account of Riis's texts is incomplete without consideration of those moments when an immigrant mother surfaces whose monstrosity clearly echoes nativist arguments and images. In *How the Other Half Lives*, Riis described two police record entries that were "far from uncommon" and pertained to "mothers in West Side tenements, who in their drunken sleep lay upon and killed their infants" (131). Similarly, his photograph "Girl and Baby on Doorstep" depicts a baby in the arms of a young girl (presumably his sister), underscoring the physical absence of the maternal figure and raising the specter of generational reproduction of inefficacious mothering. He commented that the House of Industry [an orphanage] contained "a score of babies, rescued from homes of brutality and desolation. . . . their white nightgowns hide tortured little bodies and limbs cruelly bruised by inhuman hands" (151). At such moments Riis's arguments about the deleterious effects of environment and maternal ignorance slid into an argument that constructed the heinous rather than the incapacitated immigrant mother as the cause of family breakdown. The congruence of nativist and Americanizers' representation of her at such points must be traced to their mutual investment, although differentially located, in notions of the immigrant woman's racial intractability.

If Riis's photographs convey the immigrant mother's amenability to the reformer's regulatory interventions by the docility with which she yielded herself to the lens, then the opposite effect is achieved in images such as "The Dive"

(fig. 7), which was included in both *The Battle with the Slum* and *Peril and Pres-*
ervation of the Home. Distracted by something to the left and out of the frame,
the women do not readily accede to Riis's fact-gathering mission. He typically
characterized such resistant women in terms that clearly echoed nativist thought.
They were "utterly depraved" and frequented "the borderland where the white
and black races meet in common debauch" (*How the Other Half Lives* 156).

A similar dichotomy occurred in Breckinridge's *New Homes for Old*. Embedded within a narrative largely invested in construing the foreign woman as
"Dolorosa" are immigrant women who "find themselves unequal to the task of
readjusting their lives" (52) and a particular wife who "drank and was immoral.
Instead of caring for the home and the two-year-old child, she spent her time . . .
in her brother's saloon [leaving her child]. . . . alone in the house while she went
to the 'movies'" (52–53). And in Ruth True's *The Neglected Girl,* the ineptness of
the immigrant mother in her new context slides quickly and repeatedly into an
account of her immorality: "The worry and strain of insecurity become too great
for many a woman. She grows apathetic, careless, and stolid, or she becomes
querulous and neurotic. Perhaps she takes to drink" (27). The immigrant mother

FIGURE 7. "The Dive." (The Jacob A. Riis Collection no. 346, Museum of the City of
New York)

"is spent, dragged, and worn, in pitiful need of the younger, more vigorous life at her side" (53). In this text, the proximity of mother to daughter is a danger to the latter because "the daughter of fourteen in the tenements must share the experience of the mother of fifty, who, even with the best intentions, cannot shield her girl from her own fifty-year-old materialistic morals" (78).

This facet of the Americanizers' discourse helps explain the increasing hysteria of the Americanization movement during and immediately following the war years. John Higham has argued that the period witnessed the victory of the coercive, nationalist approach of groups such as the Daughters of the American Revolution and the 100 percent Americanism movement over the more meliorative, liberal approach of those settlement workers and social reformers who stressed an educative and humanitarian approach to Americanization. My argument has suggested that the movement may not have been, in its aims, essentially bifurcated. It was the logic of the Americanizers' particular form of racialism rather than the victory of one impulse over another that led to the extreme coercion and xenophobia of their later activities.[31] The hysteria that accompanied Americanizers' activities during the war years resulted from the reformers' assumptions about the obdurate traditionalism of the immigrant woman. Such feminine intractability issued, at best, in an un-Americanized second generation and at worst in a generational schism liable to produce criminal sons and wayward daughters.

5

Eternal Mothers:
Cultural Pluralism, Primitivism,
and the Triumph of Difference

The scholar has already pointed out to us the sweetness and
charm which inhere in primitive domestic customs. . . . Something
of the same quality may be found among many of the immigrants;
when one stumbles upon an old Italian peasant with her distaff against
her withered face and her pathetic old hands patiently holding the
thread, as has been done by myriads of women since children needed
to be clad. . . . These primitive habits . . . are to be found in American
cities every day, . . a wonderful factor for poesy in cities frankly given
over to industrialism.

—Jane Addams, "Immigration"

If they become more like us, what obscure things will happen to
their souls, and if they do not, what things will happen to ours?

—Randolph Bourne

As WILLA CATHER's *O Pioneers!* (1913) draws to a close, the narrator contemplates the prospect of the immigrant protagonist's definitive assimilation and waxes elegiac. In a disconcertingly graphic passage, the narrator imag-
ines Alexandra's final "conversion": "Fortunate country, that is one day to receive
hearts like Alexandra's into its bosom, to give them out again in the yellow wheat"
(180). Even in death the immigrant remains a public asset, her significance inhering in her continued capacity to augment her adopted country's gross national
product.[1] Cather has insisted throughout on the immigrant's economic perti-
nence. By the beginning of Book Two, Alexandra's speculative and managerial
abilities have given rise not only to her own and her brothers' thriving farms but
also to an extensive infrastructure.[2] The narrator draws attention to the "tele-
phone wires [that] hum. . . . [and] light steel windmills [that] tremble" (45)
across the plains, both the product of and figure for the tensile strength and con-

centrated energy of the immigrants themselves. Unlike Trina, Alexandra does not neglect her responsibility to consume. Although personally disinterested in such matters, she dutifully "put herself into the hands of the Hanover furniture dealer, and he had conscientiously done his best to make her dining-room look like his display window" (58).

In its avowal of the link between the nation's and the immigrants' smooth rise to affluence, Cather's first novel-length treatment of immigrants in Nebraska appears to counter the logic of nativist economists. Ross's *Old World in the New* appeared a year later and warned of the socioeconomic cataclysm being fostered by the alien influx. Because *O Pioneers!* demonstrates that it is precisely the immigrants' innate (racial) qualities that guarantee both their own and the nation's prosperity, however, the novel does not so much counter as borrow that racial-economic logic to rehabilitate its immigrant characters. But perhaps rehabilitation was not quite Cather's intent. Considering the fetish made of Alexandra's whiteness throughout the narrative—the narrator repeatedly draws attention both to her Nordic heritage and to her skin, which "is of such smoothness and whiteness . . . skin with the freshness of the snow itself" (53)—the novel finally must be seen to replicate the arguments of Ross and others.[3] In other words, Alexandra is financially successful, and her assimilation proceeds seamlessly because she is of the right stock.[4]

It would be another five years before Cather moved away from this nativist paradigm. Writing in a context in which the two major formulations of the cultural-pluralist ideal had already appeared (Horace Kallen's "Democracy *versus* the Melting Pot" in 1915 and Randolph Bourne's "Trans-National America" in 1916), and perhaps responding also to the virulent chauvinism and intensified Americanization drive of the war years, Cather wrote *My Ántonia* (1918), her first cultural-pluralist treatment of immigration.[5] Like *O Pioneers!* its setting is the Nebraska prairie. Its central character is a new immigrant—a Bohemian woman. Just as Alexandra's progressive assimilation had been triumphantly heralded, Ántonia's ultimate refusal to so conform is likewise endorsed by Jim Burden, *My Ántonia*'s narrator. When Ántonia tells him "'and then, I've forgot my English so,'" he complacently notes that "the little ones [her children] could not speak English at all" (216).

Imagined proleptically, Alexandra's significance is instrumental in the nation's modernization; framed retrospectively, Ántonia's is spiritual rather than material. Her farm is a pastoral rather than an economic setting, and Ántonia herself is a product of Jim's nostalgia-drenched reminiscences. Most important, Ántonia's national contribution, like Alexandra's, is a product of her cultural (i.e., racial) identity, but that is manifest in her maternal and nurturing capacities rather than in her economic performance. *My Ántonia* is a cultural-pluralist text not because it asserts that the immigrant is nationally indispensable but because of the particular way it construes that fundamental worth.

There were distinct differences of opinion among cultural pluralists as to the origin and nature of immigrant difference and in their corresponding views of the role that ethnic groups would ideally play within a reconfigured nation. Pluralists such as Horace Kallen and Fannie Hurst relied on biological essentialism in their accounts of the origin of cultural difference. Notoriously, Kallen avowed that it was possible to change one's spouse or clothes but not one's grandfather.[6] Pluralists, however, more usually inflected the term *culture* in an essentialist direction. Jane Addams and Randolph Bourne, for example, saw difference as inhering in the immigrants' particular traditions and folkways and saw the need to nurture and protect those customs from attrition in the New World. Those differences issued in distinct concepts of the future nation. Whereas Kallen's cultural federalism envisioned the persistence of discrete cultural groups united by economic and political institutions, Bourne's more syncretic "cosmopolitan ideal" imagined that the most desirable values and customs of the immigrants would gradually infuse the entire body politic.

Ultimately, however, both pluralist visions were grounded in racial essentialism. Stephen Steinberg has shown that pluralists mounted culturally determined explanations of immigrant behavior that were every bit as essentialist as sociobiological explanations. Walter Benn Michaels has argued that the pluralist deployment of the term *culture* always occludes the racial basis on which its theory of identity depends. Pluralists construe "difference in cultural instead of political (and in addition to) racial terms" (*Our America* 11). Thus, pluralists reintroduce racial essentialism into their understanding of the origins of difference by "*deriving* . . . one's beliefs and practices *from* one's cultural identity" rather than "equating one's beliefs . . . with one's cultural identity (16, emphasis in the original).[7]

All of the cultural pluralists elaborated narratives of racial "domestication" in which the immigrant mother was key. I intend the term *racial domestication* in two senses.[8] First, pluralists conceived the influence of aliens' difference as being confined to the private and civic spheres (culturalism). Second, pluralists equated immigrants' culturally based proclivities with the values of the domestic sphere as traditionally defined, thereby producing a normative description of the immigrants' difference. Figured once more as conservative, tradition-bound, family-oriented, and fecund, these traits—to the extent that their national ramifications were corraled within the private sphere—endowed immigrants with a starring role in the pluralists' national or "trans-national" ideology.

Somewhat predictably, the immigrant mother emerges as the exemplary figure in this narrative of racial domestication. Nativists and Americanizers had largely focused on the immigrant woman within the domestic sphere in order to establish that her racial difference would inevitably leech into the very bedrock of the nation's economic and political institutions. By contrast, pluralists' texts repeatedly depict the atavistic woman functioning competently within the public sphere in order to deny that contaminating effect. Their privatization of the immigrants' difference is typically achieved through a portrayal of the foreign woman as a primitive avatar as well as a waged laborer. For example, Ántonia, although gradually elevated to the status of primitive earth mother during the course of *My Ántonia,* is depicted toiling in the fields and especially in the kitchens of others. The second and longest section of the novel is explicitly entitled "The Hired Girls." And, while *O Pioneers!* uses depictions of the heroine's labor to confirm the connection between pecuniary endeavors and racial identity, *My Ántonia*—no less invested in normative accounts of immigrant specificity—employs such representations to definitively disavow any such association. Pluralists disarticulated the realm of culture from that of the economy and reified racial difference. Their texts foreclose any consideration of the link between racialization and economic imperatives.[9] The figure of the atavistic laboring mother proves indispensable in the performance of this double movement.

My analysis of the complex role played by the immigrant mother within early pluralist texts pursues one further issue: the connection between the pluralists' construal and obsessive recycling of the immigrant woman's cultural identity as a species of primitive maternalism and the needs of the national labor market. Domestic service (the almost exclusive province of immigrant and African American women) had become a particularly dense site of racial and cultural conflict during this period.[10] Within this context, it is significant that Cather's pluralist-inspired *My Ántonia* presents the heroine's aptitude for domestic service as a product of her innate mothering proclivities ("We were singing rhymes to tease Ántonia while she was beating up one of Charley's favorite cakes in her big mixing-bowl" [103]). In other words, this chapter also pursues the connection between the pluralists' reification of the immigrant woman's putative cultural atavism and the material exploitation of the foreign woman's labor within the economy at large.

"Not the Shimerdas' Cornfields, or Mr. Bushy's, but the World's"

Although not necessarily antirestrictionist, cultural pluralism emerged during the second decade of the twentieth century as the one comprehensive argument presenting the immigrants' specificity as a valuable national resource to be fostered.[11] Such a claim entailed uncoupling the immigrants' racial traits from the specter of socioeconomic cataclysm. That link had been driven home by racial economists as early as the 1890s and was increasingly affirmed, although treated as potentially ameliorable, by Americanizers. During the immediate prewar and war years the association became entirely naturalized and elicited widespread public alarm. Accordingly, the period witnessed increased interest in Americanization projects as a means of warding off this impending disaster, and in 1917 nativists achieved a major legislative victory. The Immigration Act passed that year made admission to the United States contingent upon the payment of an $8 head tax and successful completion of a literacy test. The latter provision had been sought by both racial economists and organized labor for almost three decades.

Within this context, the work of pluralists presented the immigrants' racial attributes as having no purchase on, and therefore as incapable of infecting and vitiating, the nation's economic and political infrastructure. Pluralists construed immigrants' attributes as a matter of "emotional and involuntary life" (Kallen 124) characteristically manifested in aesthetic and expressive forms of cultural life. Arguing that immigrants' difference was derived from and exhibited in culture, they conceived the cultural and economic realms to be mutually exclusive.

Horace Kallen's "Democracy *versus* the Melting Pot," an explicit rebuttal of Ross's *Old World in the New,* was the first comprehensive statement of the cultural-pluralist ideal and a key text in the domestication of the immigrants' difference. Kallen argued that the immigrant's assimilation to the economic and political mainstream was inevitable. The demands of "rapid transit and industrial mobility" (84) made it imperative for a foreign worker to learn English, while, in turn, its acquisition meant the absorption of the "ideals that are felt to belong with the language" (85). Assimilation ensured that "the political and economic life of the commonwealth" would always remain "a single unit" (124). Kallen's argument, which assumed that an alien would discard a particular set of economic and political behaviors and acquire another, explicitly acknowledged that those behaviors were themselves culturally determined and determining. Assimilation meant that the immigrant would have to learn to "utter . . . his life in the English language and *behav[e] like an American* in matters economic and political" (115, emphasis added). It was precisely the imperative to assimilate, along with the racial prejudice encountered in the workplace, which produced the alien's preoccupation with ethnic identity: "It is the . . . feeling of aliency reenforced by social discrimination and economic exploitation that generate[s] in them [the immigrant group] an intenser group-consciousness, which then militates against 'Americanization'" (102). As this group-consciousness develops, "The arts, life and ideals of [the immigrant's own] nationality become central and paramount" (114–15). Here, Kallen presents a culturalist conception of immigrant identity as imperative in the interests of national comity. By default, the private and civil spheres become the arenas in which the expression of the immigrants' difference is contained. Further, that difference is not presented as the inevitable effect of an innate cultural or biological essence but as a formation cobbled together in the face of, and serving as a valuable resource against, racially legitimated economic exploitation.

Kallen's essay, however, simultaneously moves along a radically divergent and considerably more reactionary trajectory that presents economic and cultural practices as entirely discrete. The move ultimately proves dominant in his own argument and was replicated in the work of successive pluralists, including Bourne, Cather, and Hurst. Concomitantly, Kallen's reasoning, initially based on a theory of racial formation and construction, shifts into the rhetoric of essence. Describing the language and values imbibed by the immigrant as the mere "externals" (97) of life, Kallen argues that assimilation achieved within the public sphere precipitates the emergence of the immigrant's "intrinsic" (122) or "internal" (94) identity. Just as the acquisition of an "external" language and ideals was inevitable, so, too, was the fact that these could never impinge on the immigrants' "inward bases" (97) of national consciousness. Kallen's characterization of this consciousness (94) as "inalienable" and "a psycho-physical inheritance" (122) replicates the essentialist language of his nativist peers.[12] He departs radically from both nativists and Americanizers, however, when he argues that the expression of this "inward base" is not just manifest but contained within each individual's "emotional and involuntary life" and within each group's "peculiar dialect or speech, its own individual and inevitable esthetic and intellectual forms" (124).

In other words, Kallen's spatial conception of the immigrant's identity—consisting of an external, mutable self and an inner, inalienable racial self—also informs his conception of the respective forums in which these aspects manifest themselves. Inalienable difference is exercised solely in the realm of culture, with the latter now, by definition, unable to impinge on the macro level of politics or economics. This culturalist view of immigrant identity is presented as a normative description rather than as a pragmatic imperative enjoined upon the alien. By implication, the economic and political realms float free of the cultural determination Kallen had earlier imputed to them and acquire an immanent logic.

My Ántonia, published two years after Kallen's essay appeared in *The Nation*, embraces his vision of a homogeneous economic and political structure underwriting the proliferation of distinct and peacefully coexisting cultural communities. Like Kallen, *My Ántonia* assumes the inevitability of that development while presenting radically divergent rationales for it. Initially, Cather depicts cultural and economic behavior as reciprocally determining. Her Bohemian characters' assimilation to dominant economic conventions is understood to be the price exacted for tolerance of what, accordingly, become merely domestic peculiarities. The narrator points out that "the Shimerdas were the first Bohemian family to come to this part of the county" (15), and their unusual customs immediately elicit hostility from Jim's family. When they return the antagonism in kind, the conflict quickly escalates into physical violence. Initially, they garner animosity on every front. Their religious practices seem abhorrent, and their cultural traditions appear strange and threatening. Tales of their unsanitary culinary habits circulate widely. Consequently, Jim's grandmother quickly jettisons Mrs. Shimerda's gift of wild mushrooms: "We could not determine whether they were animal or vegetable. . . . She threw the package into the stove" (52).

Initially, too, the Bohemians' efforts at farming founder, a failure Jim imputes to an irritating inability, derived from their feudal origin, to grasp the basic capitalist laws of economic conduct: "There never were such people as the Shimerdas for wanting to give away everything they had" (29). The initial chapters repeatedly link the Shimerdas' cultural origins to their economic behavior and underscore the antagonism that the latter incites in Jim and his family. When Grandfather Burden presents Mrs. Shimerda with a cow, she—to the embarrassment of the Americans present—"crouch[ed] down beside grandfather . . . took his hand and kissed it" (87). And when the seven-year-old Ántonia offers Jim a ring in token of their friendship he "repulse[s] her quite sternly" (19), commenting that it was "no wonder Krajiek got the better of these people, if this was how they behaved" (20). As for the mother, Jim reports that she, too, "was always offering me things," adding acidly that "I knew she expected substantial presents in return" (29). Most alarmingly of all, the Shimerdas fail to evince due respect for the property rights of others. The internecine warfare between the families comes to a head when Ambrosch returns, under duress, a borrowed horse-collar that "had been badly used—trampled in the dirt and gnawed by rats" (83).

Gradually, however, the Shimerdas absorb the tenets of possessive individualism and learn to manipulate the principles of market exchange ("That cow not give so much milk like what your Grandpa say. If he make talk about fifteen dollars, I send him back the cow" [81]). Under the guidance of Grandfather Burden the Shimerdas' farming ventures flourish. Only Marek, the idiot brother, fails to throw off those feudal attitudes that prevent the acquisition of properly entrepreneurial habits ("The one idea that had ever got through poor Marek's thick head was that all exertion was meritorious" [85]). Later, Ántonia is employed by the Harling family, and this is roundly approved of as a further means of inducting both her and her family into appropriate economic and labor practices. Astutely, she forecasts the edifying effect of this opportunity: "Maybe I be the kind of girl you like better, now I come to town" (100). Thus these early chapters demonstrate that the Shimerdas must relinquish their culturally inflected economic behavior as a necessary preliminary to the achievement of the plural-

ist ideal. Jim's later, lyrical celebration of Ántonia's domesticated cultural practices testifies to the Shimerdas' ultimate success in learning to "behav[e] like . . .
an American in matters economic and political."

In its frank acknowledgment of the quid pro quo involved in the foreigner's
immigration to the United States, Cather's novel—like the initial impulse of
Kallen's argument—replicates the logic underpinning one particular provision
of the 1917 immigration bill. That legislation, registering the effects of a widespread belief that immigrants were anarchists and socialists, allowed the government to deport aliens who had radical politics and made it abundantly clear that
the admittance and continued toleration of aliens was dependent on their willingness to renounce their particular, culturally determined, economic and political beliefs.[13] It had its most spectacular effects in the years bracketing the
publication of *My Ántonia*. In 1917 Emma Goldman, the prominent immigrant
radical, and Alexander Berkman, the would-be assassin of capitalist mogul (and
immigrant) Andrew Carnegie, were arrested; both were deported in 1919.

On another level, however, Cather's narrative—like the dominant argument
in Kallen's essay—suggests that the legislative provision is entirely redundant.
Cather also portrays the public sphere—especially the realm of economic endeavor—as immune to the effects of cultural difference. Thus, at the height of
the Shimerda-Burden clash, Grandfather Burden predicts the inevitability and
particular mode of the conflict's resolution. In a passage that clearly bears the
stamp of authorial endorsement, Jim recalls his grandfather's invocation of the
mediating agency of economic processes: "It took a clear, meditative eye like my
grandfather's to foresee that . . . the . . . cornfields . . . would be, not the Shimerdas' cornfields, or Mr. Bushy's, but the world's . . . their yield would be one of
the great economic facts . . . which underlie all the activities of men" (88). Economic structures and the particular cultural system of which they form a part
are no longer mutually determining. Hence, the possibility that cultural
affiliations or institutionalized racism might affect the distribution of the profits
of the great yield is entirely foreclosed. The economy both grounds and transcends intranational, and even transnational, cultural differences. As the narrative progresses it will insist on that disjunction. Increasingly, the economic realm
"activate[s] . . . a pure process without a subject, whereas the cultural domain is
anchored deeply in Identity" (Radhakrishnan, "Postmodernism" 306). According to this logic, immigration no longer requires negotiation of the rules of a
novel economic order, nor need the state worry about the putative political and
economic effects of immigration, because cultural or racial identity have an
impact on private habits and domestic practices only.

Nativism and Americanization had always pointed indefatigably to the economically and politically disastrous effects of racial characteristics, and they elided

the fact that it was precisely their racialization of immigrants that rendered them an eminently exploitable and particularly valuable source of labor. Such racialization legitimated different pay scales and occupational tracks for immigrant and native workers.[14] Such arguments also obscured the fact that the immigrants' preoccupation with group identity was partly a result of racially legitimated inequities in the labor force. As San Juan puts it, immigrants "produced their own . . . cultures of resistance in the process of life-and-death-struggle" (39).[15] In other words, racializing discourses indirectly aided those industrial entrepreneurs whose greed nativists denounced publicly and repeatedly. Pluralism sequestered the effects of cultural difference within the private sphere and rendered the connection between economic imperatives and the racism (in which their own discourse was complicit) doubly opaque. Gordon and Newfield put it cogently: "Culturalism can allow for the segregation of culture from systematic social relations of power like capitalism," and this, in turn, "subjectivizes the concept of culture . . . *and* deculturalizes economic and political structures" (79).[16]

Thus, even though several pluralists—notably Fannie Hurst and Randolph Bourne—explicitly denounced the exploitation of immigrant labor, pluralism's constitutive foreclosure of the role that racialization played therein abetted that very exploitation.[17] In the same way, pluralism's culturalism also inaugurated the way for restrictionist arguments, which, based on "sheerly economic" grounds, proved more flexible than those of nativism or Americanization in their capacity to elide the racial imperative on which they nevertheless depended.

Eternal Mothers

Pluralists signaled their debt to modernism's primitivist project by presenting domesticated cultural difference as a valuable counterweight to the worst effects of the nation's modernization.[18] Kallen argued in "Americanization" that "against the architectonic and regimentation of the latter [science and industry] . . . the deep-lying cultural diversities of the ethnic groups are the strongest shield, the chief defense" (229). He contended that the immigrants' distinct cultures would act as a bulwark against the homogenizing and atomizing effects of exponential socioeconomic change. Randolph Bourne, railing against the "American culture of the cheap newspaper, the 'movies,' the popular song, the ubiquitous automobile" explained that Americanization produces only a "tame flabbiness" ("Trans-National America" 254).

The antidote to this cultural standardization could be found in the "cultural traditions of their [immigrant] homelands" (248). For settlement house founder Jane Addams, whose Hull House Industry Museum helpfully rendered aid to those immigrants who faltered in preserving their cultural traditions, the new-

comers would "spiritualiz[e] . . . our [America's] materialism" ("Immigration"
17).[19] In short, cultural pluralism shuffled the actors while recycling the key roles
and terms of nineteenth-century nationalist discourse. It took the gendered division of dual sphere ideology and remapped it using cultural coordinates. As
white middle-class women made increasing claims on the public sphere during
the early decades of the twentieth century, agitating for political representation
and higher education while embarking upon a series of professional careers, their
ability to figure as ahistorical symbols of national integrity seemed increasingly
moot. Cultural pluralism elevated the immigrants, in their private capacity, to
that newly vacated role of national figurehead of continuity, tradition, and spiritual values.

Notwithstanding their trumpeting of the merit of the newcomers' divergent
cultures, pluralists were little concerned to detail the particularity of the aliens'
ideals or describe the specific tenor of each national groups' "emotional and
involuntary life." Pluralists who followed Kallen conjured away the putative
multiplicity of immigrants' cultural practices even as they paid lip service to
them. In pluralist work after pluralist work, the invocation of multifarious traditions yields to a normative and extremely truncated list of traits shared by all
new immigrant groups. This reduction of cultural traditions and heritage to traits
is particularly evident in Randolph Bourne's "Trans-National America," when,
having invoked the value of "tenacious folk tradition[s]," he fails to provide a
sketch of those traditions.[20] Instead, he ascribes to the immigrants an overweening commitment to their heritage and construes that commitment, rather than
the heritage itself, as antimodernist in tendency. Cather and Hurst likewise produced a normative account of the immigrants' characteristics rather than a description of their diverse customs. Furthermore, across the work of all the early
pluralists the characteristics ascribed to the immigrant invariably turn out to be
coterminous with the values of the domestic sphere as traditionally conceived.
Arguing that immigrants particularly esteemed those values usually associated
with the private sphere, pluralists produced a familiar catalog of immigrant traits:
conservativism bordering on atavism, overwhelming dedication to family life and
maintainence of tradition, and a primitive vitality evidenced chiefly but not solely
in a superlative fecundity.

Not surprisingly, the primitive immigrant mother recurs across pluralist texts
as the key avatar of this domestic complex. Jane Addams's invocation of an "old
Italian peasant with her distaff against her withered face and her pathetic old
hands holding the thread" ("Immigration" 13) is entirely typical. So, too, is
Cather's characterization of her immigrant protagonist in *My Ántonia*. Cather
claimed that the novel "had as its purpose the desire to express the quality of these
[immigrant] people" and that quality is largely embodied in the earthy, vital

Ántonia, who was, Cather averred, "tied to the soil" (*Willa Cather in Person* 72). Ántonia's rootedness in the past renders her thematically and nationally significant.[21] As Cather's text modulates from its early exploration of the practices constituting the Bohemians' cultural identity into the more regressive project of limning the anterior identity grounding those divergent practices, Ántonia's significance—as incarnation of that anterior identity—grows apace. Her sentience, vigor, lack of material concerns, and devotion to her family are foregrounded against the physical and emotional barrenness of both the Americans and assimilated immigrants who surround her. In contrast to the sterility of the Burdens—Jim has no siblings, no parents, no children, and may be the last of his line—Ántonia accedes to a productive motherhood and wifehood. She provides a well of spiritual rejuvenation to which Jim, chief representative of the progressive, urban life from which Ántonia is, by novel's conclusion, definitively separated, returns again and again. She is endowed with the status of earth mother, ensconced on a remote homestead in the middle of the prairie and ultimately defined by her extensive family, number of fruit trees, and collection of pickling jars.[22]

This representation of the immigrant mother recurs across the pluralists' work and effectively conveys their newly minted conception of the immigrants' national value. The immigrant woman could only function in this way, however, to the degree that her cultural difference was definitively divorced from the realm of progress and change and positioned within "a permanently anterior time within the modern nation" (McClintock 93). Thus, the alien woman no longer— as she had in nativism and Americanization—simply embodies the immigrants' alterity. Importantly, she also functions allegorically, signaling the limits to as well as the contours of cultural difference. That double role is most readily achieved in the bulk of early pluralist texts by introducing the primitive immigrant woman into the public sphere—particularly into the labor force—in order to demonstrate her innocuousness therein. Pluralist texts make repeated and distinctive recourse to the figure of the atavistic, laboring, immigrant woman in order to sever the connection conclusively between cultural difference and socioeconomic disaster. In that respect Randolph Bourne's work is entirely representative. It is his anecdotal essay "Emerald Lake" (1917), however, rather than "Trans-National America," his classic statement of cultural-pluralist ideals, which is particularly pertinent to my argument.

"Emerald Lake" is part ethnography, part tour guide. Surveying an Italian suburb of Chicago, Bourne is initially repulsed, his rhetoric reminiscent of Stephen Crane's: "In spite of the sprawling space all about, these houses bulge with dark people. A little squalid shop usually darkens the ground floor, and from the apartments above float streamers of bright-colored clothes. . . . Black-haired babies and bristly dogs roll in the gutter and on the sidewalks where some bold entrepreneur has already laid his line of 'concrete'" (271). The women congregating on the street seem "swarthy, heavy, incorrigibly healthy. . . . all smoothly black-haired . . . they all look middle-aged and they all look alike" (271). It is the concrete, however, a reminder of the encroaching city and "shifty 'real-estate development company,'" which impels Bourne to reconsider his distaste and ponder further the "nature" of Italians. Remembering that they are an "integrated and elemental people" (272), he contemplates the women again and revises his initial impression. He decides that "illiterate and primitive as I knew them to be, . . . there is a certain piratical vigor and intensity about them" (272, 271). This vigor is manifest in their reproductive capacities: "The[ir] babies . . . give . . . evidence that these broad women are not middle-aged but the authentic mothers of them and in the full tide of their prolific career" (272). A proto-nativist construction of the immigrant mother's reproductive potency is quickly retooled to signify not a burgeoning tide of racial degeneracy but rather her ability to resist the anomic tendencies of modern life.

Simultaneously, however, Bourne demonstrates the immunity of the broader public sphere to the effects of the women's atavism. He accomplishes that by juxtaposing the first group of Italian women with a second group—their daughters—who are returning home from the mill where they are employed. Wondering if the immigrants "will . . . make us gayer, intenser, more primitive," his contemplation of the laboring daughters seems to confirm his worst expectations: "Our streets [will] merely sophisticate and corrode their vigor" (272).

Lacking their mothers' primitive vitality, Bourne fears that as a direct result of their factory work the second generation will "stay soft and foolish and fail to jump suddenly into eternal-looking mothers" (272). The oscillation between these primitive race-mothers and their foolish, assimilated daughters is critical not only because it manifests Bourne's hesitation about the tenacity of the immigrants' traits but also because the juxtaposition reconfirms the home as the space in which the effects of cultural proclivities are sequestered. The public sphere threatens that difference ("Will they remain soft and foolish? . . . will our streets corrode their vigor?") but is impervious to its effects. In the light of Kallen's argument concerning the bifurcated nature of immigrant subjectivity, one could read these mothers and daughters as complementary aspects, rather than contrasting versions, of Italian identity within the New World. The "eternal mothers" signify the cultural or inward aspect of that secondary, external, self, which, as in the case of their daughters, successfully and daily conforms to the demands of the public sphere.

In Fannie Hurst's novel *Lummox* (1923), both the inward and the external selves are combined in Bertha, the immigrant protagonist. Hurst is now best known for *Imitation of Life* (1933), which describes the relationship between an African American domestic laborer and her white female employer. During the 1920s and 1930s, however, Hurst's short stories and novels, which repeatedly mined the East Side for characters and themes, won her a national and even international reputation. She successfully targeted the popular market. As Abe Ravitz points out, she "was frequently identified as the 'highest paid writer in the world,'" and she used her celebrity and wealth to support a number of progressive causes, including "civil rights, slum clearance, and workmen's compensation" (1, 33). *Lummox* extended her popular appeal and also achieved considerable critical success, garnering high praise from, among others, an anonymous *New York Times* reviewer; from Charles Hanson Towne, the reviewer for the *International Review of Books;* and from Carl Van Doren.[23] One of the few sour notes was struck by Hamlin Garland in the *New York Times.* Garland implicated Hurst's novel in his sweeping indictment of what he perceived to be the general drift of American fiction, which was "'in process of being Europeanized,' its people and themes 'increasingly alien to our tradition'" (Ravitz 121).

Lummox is chiefly concerned with the plight of immigrant domestic servants and follows the career of Bertha, an orphan of Slavic descent raised in Brooklyn by native Americans. Her country of origin is uncertain because, as the novel's opening line runs, "Nobody quite knew just what Baltic bloods flowed in sullen and alien rivers through Bertha's veins—or cared" (1). Those origins are manifest in her primal nature—she has "luscious feet that listened to the soil and stole its secrets. A sublime kind of capillarity" (12)—and in her inexhaustible reserves of emotional and material generosity. Unable to forget "the knowledges that came to her in chimes from the dark forests within her" (2), she uses that aboriginal knowledge to nurture those native Americans she encounters with a kind of stupified and semiconscious benevolence, repaying abuse with dumb compassion.

The text is partly motivated by a desire to give voice to the immigrants' perspective on what had widely become known as the "servant problem." The narrator registers loud protest at the increasing exploitation of Bertha by a succession of employers. As housework became increasingly professionalized, domestic laborers became subject to "the same forms of control as factory workers, including the standardization of work procedures and speedups" (Romero 57). Hurst provides a graphic account of the long hours of physical labor, which, coupled with the employer's "supervisory techniques" (Romero 58) and unremitting surveillance, made domestic service a particularly unpleasant proposition.

As Bertha ages and her body weakens, she obtains ever-less-desirable positions, sliding slowly into poverty. Despite the fact that her cultural origins have led her to nurture her employers emotionally and even sexually on occasion throughout her working life, she is not protected from dismissal once her productivity wanes. Hurst's indignation at Bertha's treatment takes the form of a demand that the workplace's neutrality with respect to race be alleviated ("Nobody quite knew just what Baltic bloods flowed . . . through Bertha's veins—*or cared*" [1, emphasis added]). The novel registers outrage because Bertha's aboriginality, although manifest in the public sphere, does not and cannot have impact on the market value of her labor. In other words, *Lummox* occludes the relationship between racialization and the profit motive while reifying the racial categories that serve that motive. Although explicitly concerned with the conditions of immigrant labor, the novel forms part of a larger structure of racialization that naturalizes those conditions. In the closing pages, Hurst provides Bertha with a surrogate immigrant family. She retreats to the home, where alone she can be rewarded for her culturally mandated and nationally invaluable role of eternal mother.

My Ántonia is hardly concerned to decry exploitative labor practices, although it, too, explicitly and repeatedly invites consideration of immigrant women in their capacity as waged workers. The second section of the novel ("The Hired Girls") deals with Ántonia's move from the family farm to town, where she is employed as a domestic by the Harling family. It is framed by Jim's sociological ruminations upon the economic significance of Ántonia and the other "hired girls." He observes that immigrants, unlike the daughters of American farmers, cannot "get positions as teachers" and have "no alternative but to go into service" (128) in order to support their struggling families. A thematic space in which the connection between racialization and delimited employment options might be considered briefly opens. Domestic service was (and remains) an occupation that was particularly racially segregated. "As immigrant women entered domestic service in the North, class and racial tensions heightened and native-born women began to avoid the occupation at all costs" (Romero 77). The issue, however, is immediately turned aside as Cather's stout commitment to a bootstrapping ethic leads her to a vision of future material progress achieved by successive generations of immigrant women: "The girls who once worked in Black Hawk kitchens are to-day managing big farms . . . of their own" (128). Ultimately, though, *My Ántonia* obscures the racial-economic nexus most effectively by asking readers to celebrate the survival of the immigrant woman's cultural traits despite her immersion in the world of labor.

This overwhelmingly dominant theme is most forcefully established in the final scene of the novel, when Jim, having returned to visit Ántonia after an absence of twenty years, ruminates on the ways in which a life of hard labor has marked her physically. "How little it mattered—about her teeth, for instance" he observes (216). They matter little because, although testament to the fact that she had "lived . . . much and . . . hard" (214), she remains "in the full vigour of her personality, battered but not diminished" (214). Her "inner glow" and "fire of life" have not been sapped (216). The recognition that Ántonia's exploitation has partly been a function of her racialization is sublated by Jim's celebration of the survival of Ántonia's cultural identity despite her years of toil. Her victory represents the triumph of cultural difference as represented in her "vigor," "inner glow," and indomitable "personality." In the difficult intervening decades, it seems to Jim as though "her identity [had become] stronger" (214). Her worn body, lined face, and lack of teeth (she is only forty) are meant to signify not how racial construction legitimates exploitative labor conditions, which in turn corporally reshape the racialized subject, but the triumph of an indomitable cultural essence in the face of those conditions.

This triumphalism, in turn, is possible only because the narrative has already conclusively construed Ántonia's difference as innocuous in the context of the nation's modernizing thrust. Cather achieves that by invoking the economic sphere as a species of deus ex machina that transcends and mediates cultural conflict. More extensively, this is achieved by Ántonia's particular occupation—domestic service—as well as by the novel's specific mode of representing that occupation. Domestic service had long been seen by Americanizers as an important avenue by which immigrant women could imbibe "middle-class values, particularly work-discipline" (Romero 61).[24] Certainly, Mrs. Harling sees domestic service in this light. Upon her decision to hire Ántonia, she confidently asserts, "I can bring something out of that girl. She's . . . not too old to learn new ways" (99).

Of course, Mrs. Harling is entirely mistaken in that assumption, because Ántonia proves to have little to learn from her mistress. On the contrary, from the beginning there is "a basic harmony between" them (115). Both "loved children and animals and music, and rough play and digging in the earth. They liked to prepare rich, hearty food . . . to make up soft white beds " (116). Domestic service requires precisely those innate traits Cather imputes to the immigrant: a maternal penchant, an earthiness, and an elemental vigor. Accordingly, Ántonia describes her period of domestic service as being "'like Heaven'" (113). Jim enthusiastically notes that "she was never too tired to make taffy . . . for us. . . . Tony would rush into the kitchen and build a fire in the range on which she had already cooked three meals that day" (113). The implication is that this labor is no labor at all.[25] It requires only that Ántonia manifest that elemental maternalism that is the sign and product of her cultural identity. By the same token, this worksite is devoid of cultural conflict, not because Ántonia assimilates to its demands but because its requirements are precisely those to which she is innately fitted. That is doubly ironic because not only is domestic service inextricable from "the capitalism that produced and continues to maintain a gender stratified and racially hierarchical labor market" (Romero 93) but also because "race relations and domestic service" were inextricably intertwined at the cusp of the last century. Thus, "racial and cultural differences between employees and employers were so apparent that the 'servant problem' became synonymous with more general social conflicts over ethnicity, race, or religion" (Romero 77). Cather's narrative transforms what was an occupation striated by race and subject to internecine racial and cultural conflict into a collective engagement in maternal nurturing, and it construes the immigrant woman as essentially suited, by way of her culture (i.e., her race), to such an occupation.

By contrast, those immigrant women who venture into different forms of employment lose their invaluable difference and "fail to jump suddenly into eternal-looking mothers." The figure against whom Ántonia's "triumph" is measured is Lena. Also a second-generation immigrant raised on the farm, Lena puts her dressmaking talents to work, establishes herself in business, and eventually becomes financially successful. Her ensuing loss of vitality is underscored: Lena is "quietly conventionalized by city clothes" (170). Jim explicitly compares Lena's ready transformation with Ántonia's resolute alterity: "Ántonia had never talked like the people about her. Even after she learned to speak English readily, there was always something impulsive and foreign in her speech. But Lena had picked up all the conventional expressions she heard" (180). Lena's assimilation renders her lethargic. She has a "sleepy smile" and a "lazy, good-natured laugh" (109,108), and, like the other immigrant businesswomen in the novel, she ends up single, childless, and, by implication, lonely. Her friend Tiny Soderball, who makes a fortune in mining speculation, is described as one "in whom the faculty of becoming interested is worn out" (194). In this, Tiny recalls both Jim's wife, from whom Jim is disaffected (she is "temperamentally incapable of enthusiasm"), as well as the native town girls, "whose muscles seemed to ask but one thing—not to be disturbed" (128).

Cather's narrative, despite its constitutive occlusion of the connection between racism and economic exploitation, surreptitiously reintroduces racial considerations into the public sphere by indexing the immigrants' value to their retention of particular kinds of menial employment. That indexing remains relatively implicit in My Ántonia, although it is clearly articulated in Randolph Bourne's "Emerald Lake." Bourne's juxtaposition of the soft and foolish factory girls with their elemental mothers raises the question of whether it might be in the national interest to retain immigrants in occupations that would insulate them against the loss of their primitive vitality. As he contemplates a group of Italian ditchdiggers, Bourne wonders, "If they surrender ditch digging. . . . will there be provided for them or will they create for themselves work that will keep all that elemental vigor?" (272). He forecasts and deplores the men's transformation into "the painfully collared Domenicoes who stand around the saloon of an evening" (272).

Bourne's narrative of domestication—like Cather's—conveys both the innocuousness and the tenuousness of the immigrants' difference within the public sphere. Both texts reintroduce into that sphere cultural considerations previously expunged in order to mount an argument for the immigrant's ideal menial employment. Drawing upon the immigrant woman in order to underscore the immigrant's autocthony, pluralists no longer linked her primitive essence to national cataclysm; instead they parlayed that essence into an argument for the alien's peculiar value. And that value, across the pluralists' body of work, is directly indexed to the immigrants' retention within poorly remunerated and nonprofessional forms of labor.

Conclusion

IT SEEMS CLEAR that in the three decades leading up to the passage of the Johnson-Reed Act, nativists' particular framing of the immigration issue acquired a hegemonic status that neither Americanizers nor pluralists ever seriously threatened. Although progressive reformers and social workers provided influential counternarratives, nativists grasped the discursive offensive early and never relinquished that advantage. Certainly, nativists proved adept at disseminating their views, gaining access to a wide variety of media throughout the period. That success, however, was itself contingent upon the cultural resonance of their particular version of the immigrant problem. Indeed, not even the texts of those whose political convictions placed them in a different camp proved entirely immune from its influence. The success of any hegemonic formulation lies, as Raymond Williams reminds, not just in its ability to render its particular interpretation of events dominant but in its ability to "neutraliz[e], chang[e] or actually incorporat[e]" oppositional initiatives (114). By that measure, nativism clearly achieved hegemonic status, the counternarratives of Americanization and pluralism both periodically yielding to the nativists' particular version of racialization. The assimilative optimism of Riis and other progressives waned quickly when faced with resistant foreign mothers, while Kallen's and Hurst's pluralism drew upon the biological accounts of cultural difference endemic to nativist thought. In other words, nativism formed the discursive horizon against which the immigration issue was framed and considered at the turn of the nineteenth century. Nowhere, perhaps, is that more evident than in the fact that both Americanizers and pluralists waged their rhetorical counteroffensives around and through the already densely scripted figure of the alien mother. While the place of the immigrant woman within these texts was linked to the Americanizers' and pluralists' particular social convictions, it is also the case that her reconstruction was politically imperative if nativism were to be effectively combated.

Yet the concepts of oppositionality and rapprochement are not ultimately sufficient to grasp the relationships that obtained between these racializing narratives. With respect to the cultural work performed by pluralism and nativism, these discourses appear, rather, as necessary complements. The ultimate success of nativist campaigns always proved counterproductive in that they shut off the labor supply that their own discourse of racialization had helped keep inexpensive. The immediate result of the 1917 immigration bill, in tandem with U.S. entry into the war, was the development of a severe labor deficit. The ninth provision of that bill anticipated such a predicament, however, allowing for the setting aside of any of the bill's requirements should a labor shortage develop in any particular economic sector (Cardoso 47). Despite nativist rhetoric, it was abundantly clear that U.S. agricultural and industrial interests were dependent on immigrant labor as "railroad, mining, and industrial interests pleaded" for the setting aside of the literacy provision for some alien workers (47). Accordingly, in May 1917 the secretary of labor exempted Mexican agricultural workers from the head tax and literacy test imposed by the bill, and in July 1918 the exemption was extended to nonagricultural workers (48). Cultural pluralism's narrative of racial domestication was more flexible and responsive to the nation's industrial needs. Like nativism, it racialized and hence stratified the labor force, but unlike nativism it did not require the cessation of this flow of cheap labor. Thus, where its arguments seemed most at odds with contemporaneous racialisms, pluralism replicated nativism's cultural work.[1]

The story I have told concerning the racialization of the immigrant woman at the turn of the nineteenth century is significant in that it constitutes a notable episode in a stubbornly persistent American saga of racialization. It is, perhaps, especially critical to examine this racializing rhetoric from the vantage point of the 1990s, in which the resurgence of nativism among groups of diverse political persuasions has been nurtured and its specific contours inflected by the economic shift toward post-Fordism.

When I began this book in 1989, my interest in the role of the immigrant woman within the turn-of-the-century debate over immigration was primarily a historical one, albeit undoubtedly informed by my own position as a resident alien. As I continued work on the manuscript, however, the issue of immigration once again began to garner widespread national concern and the similarities between the rhetoric deployed in both periods became more and more apparent. That reanimated anxiety has issued in, to name only some of the more notorious incidents, the passage of Proposition 187 in California (1994); the publication of the Recommendations of the Commission on Immigration Reform, chaired by Barbara Jordan (1995); and the passage of the Personal Responsibility Work Opportunity Act, which included provisions rendering legal immigrants ineligible for SSI and food stamps (1996).[2] Meanwhile, popular contemporary treatments of immigration, such as Brent Nelson's *America Balkanized* (1995) and Peter Brimelow's *Alien Nation: Common Sense about America's Immigration Disaster* (1995), echo the racializing discourse of the earlier period, although of course the focus of racial animus has shifted along with the natal origins of the chief immigrant groups. Nelson warns of the rise of the "Tex-Mex nation," and Brimelow, the senior editor at *Forbes,* also cautions against the sociocultural impact of the influx of Latino workers. "Americans," he argues, are being "robbed . . . of the power to determine who and how many, can enter their national family" (4–5).

The contemporary debate over immigration also focuses on the figure of the immigrant woman, although perhaps not quite so intensively as the previous controversy.[3] As I noted in the Introduction, the 1993 *Time* special issue on America's genetic future clearly expresses racial anxiety in its account of the morph program's malfunction and production of a grotesque female figure. That figure displaces what the magazine insinuates about the immigrant woman: that her reproductive capacities are potentially monstrous. Similarly, Brimelow explicitly inveighs against the preternatural fecundity of Latina immigrants and holds that immigrants "seem to have children at a faster pace than the native-born Americans" (44). Replicating century-old arguments about the imminent danger of race suicide, he warns that *"two-thirds* of the births in Los Angeles County hospitals are to illegal-immigrant mothers" (4, emphasis in the original) and points to a survey "of new Hispanic mothers in California border hospitals [which] found that 15 percent had crossed the border specifically to give birth" (4). Accordingly, he advocates, as part of a larger immigration reform package, "reviving a version of the *bracero* program" (266) and permitting only immigration by skilled laborers who are male and single. Historian and critic Leo Chavez has pointed out that "the first action Governor Wilson took after passage of Proposition 187 was to move to cut off prenatal care to undocumented women" (71). Indeed, Chavez argues that this proposition "target[s] reproduction—predominantly women and children" (69). Chavez contends that the current wave of anti-immigrant legislation is not designed to stop the "production-work of immigrant labor" (69). Rather, it is specifically contrived to ensure that the United States will not have to bear the costs of reproducing the labor it continues to exploit: "By targeting reproduction, immigrant reform does very little to undermine the lucrative and highly profitable relation between employers and workers" (70).

The contemporary fomentation of nativist hysteria not only does "little to undermine" that relation, but, as in the previous moment, it also directly abets it.[4] Tracking the discursive production of the racialized immigrant woman at the moment of capital's last major reorganization has thrown into relief the similar fomentation of anxiety around that figure in a contemporary setting. One can hope that the link between corporate greed and socioeconomic upheaval will not be so effectively elided this time around. As the ongoing effects of economic globalization and corporate downsizing ripple through the culture, however, it remains to be seen whether the recruitment of that perennially serviceable icon, the atavistic alien woman, will once again succeed in obscuring the common interests of immigrant and indigenous workers.

Notes

Introduction

1. These groupings are: Middle-Eastern, Italian, African, Vietnamese, Anglo-Saxon, Chinese, and Hispanic. Michael Rogin provides an intriguing interpretation of this *Time* issue in *Blackface, White Noise*, also relating it to early-twentieth-century eugenic anxieties. He cites the detail of the morph program's malfunction as a manifestation of contemporary racialist anxieties and analyzes the magazine's paradoxical elision of blackness in the projected national physiognomy. He also points out that the seven "racial types" identified by the article do not include the category of the African American (only the term *African* appears), while all the non-Caucasian figures are "whitened" (6–8). Rogin does not, however, deal with the particular significance of the sex of the morph and cover image.

For an extended consideration of the links between contemporary nativism and its historical antecedents in the United States, see *Immigrants Out!* edited by Juan Perea, especially Joe Feagin, "Old Poison in New Bottles" (chapter 2).

2. I will be using the term *nativist* in two senses. Following John Higham, I use the term to refer, in its largest sense, to anti-immigrant sentiment. Nativism, understood in this way, consists of three components: "the anti-Catholic, anti-radical, and Anglo-Saxon" (*Strangers* 11). I am concerned in this book with the last strand, which entails the racialization of the immigrant. Within the attempt to racialize the foreigner, there were, in turn, three major positions: that of the biological or scientific racists (in standard usage, dubbed "nativists"), who saw difference as inhering in genetics; that of the Americanizers, who saw it as stemming from environment or inhering in culture; and that of the cultural pluralists, who saw it as a function of culture and/or genetics but in either case welcomed the foreigner's racial difference. I am indebted to Stow Persons, *Ethnic Studies at Chicago*, which contains a succinct account of the various positions within the debate and identifies some of the key proponents of each.

3. Higham's *Strangers* remains the definitive work on anti-immigrant sentiment in the nineteenth and early twentieth centuries. I am deeply indebted to his account and analysis of nativism's rise.

4. Work addressing the convergence of race and maternity in nineteenth- and twentieth-century American culture has begun to proliferate. Laura Doyle's *Bordering on the Body* focuses on that intersection in order to read a series of modernist American and European novels. In *That Pale Mother Rising* Eva Cherniavsky examines the intersection of maternal and racial identities in a series of nineteenth-century American texts, as does Stephanie Smith in *Conceived by Liberty*. Specific discussions of the articulation of race at the site of the African American maternal body are also numerous and include Diane Roberts, *The Myth of Aunt Jemima*, the final chapter of Dana Nelson, *The Word in Black and White*, and K. Sue Jewell, *From Mammy to Miss America and Beyond*. Hortense Spillers's "Mama's Baby, Papa's Maybe" provides the analytical point of departure for many of these works.

5. I take the term *unruly* from Mary Russo's Bakhtinian-inspired *The Female Grotesque*.

6. Again, I follow Laclau and Mouffe in stressing the political nature of representational struggle; see *Hegemony and Socialist Strategy*, especially chapters 3 and 4.

7. For example, in his discussion of contemporary British racisms, Gilroy discriminates between the new racists, who evoke culture and identity in their work, and more traditional British racists (exemplified by Enoch Powell and others like him) who use biological accounts of racial difference (43 passim).

8. I draw the term *racial-ethnic* from Bonnie Thornton Dill; see "Our Mother's Grief."

9. By contrast, Frank Norris certainly seems to have held nativist views.

10. The term *cultural work* is Jane Tompkins's; see *Sensational Designs*, xv passim.

11. In *Strangers*, Higham has taken up this question of nativism's popular purchase. He clearly indicates that popular nativism tended to ebb and flow across the period and contends that during the late 1890s nativist rhetoric found a particularly receptive popular audience: The depression of 1893 through 1897 helped nativism to spread "nationwide" (73). By the early years of the twentieth century, however, popular nativism attenuated, a period Higham sees as one in which optimistic, assimiliationist views of the immigrant issue spread more widely (109–11). By about 1910, though, opinion again shifted, and popular nativism burgeoned. That sentiment, exacerbated by America's entry into the war and the perceived need for "100 percent Americanization," continued unabated until the 1920s.

12. I have also concentrated on the texts produced by a sociocultural elite largely self-identified as "Anglo-Saxon." Of course, immigrant women were far from mute during these years. They produced a large body of texts, and such writers as Mary Antin, Anzia Yezierska, Emma Goldman, and Elizabeth Stern, to mention but a very few, became well know for their biographical and fictional renditions of their personal immigrant experiences. Work is beginning to accrete around immigrant women's texts, especially the autobiographies published during this period; among them are Anne E. Goldman, *Take My Word* and Magdalena Zaborowoska, *How We Found America*. My focus and interest, however, is on the modes of representation that a dominant group produced about a culturally marginal group.

13. As has often been pointed out, that process was aided by the fact that the late 1890s saw a marked shift in the natal origin of immigrants from Northwestern Europe to Southern and Eastern Europe. The latter groups (Slavs, Jews, and Italians) came gradually to be seen as one entity (the new immigration) as opposed to the old immigration from Northern Europe. See Higham, *Strangers,* chapters 4 and 7, for an extended discussion. What is clear from the literature of the period, however, is the extent to which this xenophobia eventually spilled over to affect even those immigrant groups—such as the Irish—which had earlier been rehabilitated, or reclaimed for whiteness. The extent to which the Irish immigrant woman recurs within racializing discourses at the end of the century suggests a need to rethink analyses, which, attending to the process whereby the Irish gradually become recognized as white during the nineteenth century, pinpoint that reclamation as having been decisively achieved by the 1870s.

14. This compares with 59.6 percent between 1820 and 1867 (United States Immigration Commission 59). These are overall figures; the proportion of male to females varied widely according to natal origin.

15. See, among many other discussions, Radhakrishnan, "Nationalism, Gender, and the Narrative of Identity."

16. See, among others, Mary Ryan, *Empire of the Mother;* Nancy Cott, *The Bonds of Womanhood;* Gillian Brown, *Domestic Individualism;* Stephanie Smith, *Conceived by Liberty;* Hazel Carby, *Reconstructing Womanhood;* and Eva Cherniavsky, *That Pale Mother Rising.*

17. As Laura Mulvey observes, "It is the mother who guarantees the privacy of the home by maintaining its respectability, as essential a defence against outside incursion or curiosity as the encompassing walls of the home itself" (69).

18. See the work of Lauren Berlant, who in *Anatomy of National Fantasy* analyzes the place of the white woman's body within the "National Symbolic," a collectively held fantasy about the nation's parameters and substance (20 passim).

19. Stephanie Smith illustrates how the vision of true womanhood limned in Lydia Maria Child's *The Mother's Book* is haunted by a necessary inverse. "Repeatedly locat[ing] excess as a female trait while calling on females to be the guardians of restraint" (61). Child's text is paradigmatic of a larger national anxiety concerning the over-invested figure of the reproductive woman.

20. Doyle, *Bordering on the Body,* deals chiefly with modernist fiction and also attends to the articulation of race at the site of the mother's body within early-twentieth-century culture, identifying the critical role that eugenics played therein. Doyle does not discriminate, however, between the racialization of the black as opposed to the immigrant mother and uses an anthropological framework—a "theory of kinship patriarchy"—to explain the general tendency to articulate maternity and race: "Under kinship patriarchy women are both central and marginal in that they serve the central role of creating the group's margins. At the symbolic level the figure of the mother reproduces a racialized cultural discourse" (27). By contrast, my analysis of the immigrant mother-race articulation examines specific familial, racial, and maternal discourses circulating within late-nineteenth- and early-twentieth-century U.S. culture.

21. I am indebted to Gilroy in that he has stressed the importance of the notion of the family in constructing concepts of race and nation; see *"There Ain't No Black in the Union Jack,"* especially chapter 2. See also Walter Benn Michaels, *Our America,* for a discussion of the role of the family in nativist discourse within the U.S. context.

22. Wald's discussion of Stein in *Constituting Americans* (chapter 4) traces the articulation of family with regard to race and nation within the parameters of the discourse of Americanization. Her focus is on the writers—both immigrant and otherwise—who reveal the difficulties of the imperative to assimilate. My concern is with the place of the immigrant woman within that complex and with the different representations of pathological immigrant families that emerge within various immigrant discourses.

23. The literature on this is vast. For accounts of how this operates in the British context, see Gilroy, *"There Ain't No Black in the Union Jack,"* and Carby, "Schooling in Babylon." Within the American context, see, among many others, K. Sue Jewell, *From Mammy to Miss America;* Toni Morrison's edited collection *Race-ing Justice,* especially the essays of Paula Giddings, Wahneema Lubiano, Nell Irvin Painter, and Christine Stansell; Patricia Morton, *Disfigured Images;* and Hortense Spillers, "Mama's Baby, Papa's Maybe."

24. See Miriam King and Steven Ruggles's analysis of the empirical rationale for such fears: "American Immigration, Fertility, and Race Suicide at the Turn of the Century." They conclude that "overall, immigrants did have higher fertility than native-born women. But, when we consider the fertility of the daughters of immigrants—the 'home-grown foreigners'—the results sharply contradict both previous demographic research and the Victorian prophets of race suicide. Regardless of the measure employed . . . second-generation women had substantially lower fertility than any other group, including the native women. Such low fertility among second-generation women contradicts any simple linear relationship between assimilation and fertility control" (352). For a contemporary version of the race suicide argument, see Peter Brimelow, *Alien Nation.*

25. Painter provides a succinct account of the historical and cultural pervasiveness of these images in "Hill, Thomas, and the Power of Racial Stereotype."

26. Morton is drawing here on the work of Deborah White.

27. Morton is summarizing the work of Catherine Clinton.

28. Jewell, *From Mammy to Miss America;* Morton, *Disfigured Images.*

29. In Diane Roberts's description, "Aunt Jemima's enormous bosom signifies her maternal feeding function" (2).

30. See *Race-ing Justice,* ed. Morrison, especially the essays of Lubiano, Painter, and Stansell.

31. Roberts, *The Myth of Aunt Jemima;* Painter, "Hill, Thomas, and the Power of Racial Stereotype." As Diane Roberts puts it, "The white world drew the black woman's body as excessive and flagrantly sexual, quite different from the emerging ideology of purity and modesty which defined the white woman's body" (5). That was especially the case in the American South during the antebellum period: "In American iconography the sexually promiscuous black girl . . . represents the mirror image of the white woman on the pedestal" (Painter 207).

32. The sole exception is Maggie's mother.

33. Berlant describes the National Symbolic as "the order of discursive practices whose reign within a national space . . . transforms individuals into subjects of a collectively-held history" (20).

Chapter 1: A Rediscovered Problem

1. While Michaud located difference in blood, Ripley ascribed the initial assumption of racial difference to the influences of geography. As Gossett points out, however, he also believed that "mental and emotional qualities are inherited racially though he was much more cautious than most anthropologists of the period in describing these qualities" (413). That belief ultimately rendered his work extremely useful to biological racists such as Grant and Fairchild.

2. The term *melting pot* did not become current until 1908, when Israel Zangwill's play of the same title was produced. Stow Persons describes the beliefs and principal adherents of Anglo-American assimilationism in *Ethnic Studies at Chicago*.

3. Sklar, *The Corporate Reconstruction of American Capitalism*.

4. William Z. Ripley was an anthropologist and economist who taught at both Columbia University and MIT (Higham, *Strangers* 154–55). See Gossett, however, for a different reading of the import of Ripley's text (413).

5. In *Paddy and the Republic*, especially chapter 4, Dale Knobel includes a comprehensive discussion of the construction of the Irish as a racial category in the nineteenth-century United States.

6. See Gail Bederman's comprehensive account of how turn-of-the-century Americans "used race to remake manhood" (5) as normative gender ideals broke up under the impress of socioeconomic shifts. I am indebted to the analysis she pursues in *Manliness and Civilization*.

7. See Stephen Meyer, *The Five Dollar Day*, for a detailed account of this ceding of worker autonomy in return for waged incentives.

8. See T. J. Jackson Lears, *No Place of Grace* and "From Salvation to Self-Realization," for a comprehensive discussion of the ambivalence attending this gradual, unevenly achieved, shift.

9. See Mark Seltzer, *Bodies and Machines*, and Martha Banta, *Taylored Lives*, for accounts of the cultural impact of these shifts in production processes.

10. Haraway notes that Madison Grant was a trustee of the American Museum of Natural History.

11. See Gossett's discussion of Strong (*Race* 185–91) and Jurgen Herbst's introduction in Strong, *Our Country*.

12. As Higham has argued (*Strangers* 33), mid-nineteenth-century Anglo-Saxonism had largely been a militantly optimistic and nationalistic ideology that avowed faith in the Anglo-Saxon stock's capacity to absorb into itself the immigrant influx.

13. Bederman argues (23–31) that the yoking of Darwinism to millennial versions of history was a culturewide phenomenon during this period.

14. While in England, he became a close friend of Stephen and Cora Crane, who were also living there. Myers, *Reluctant Expatriate*, 145–49.

15. Mendel's findings concerning the inheritance of genetic traits formed the basis for the eugenic theories that underwrote nativist discourse. See Carol McCann, *Birth Control Politics in the U.S.*, for a full account of this debt. Frederic was apparently fascinated by Mendel's experiments. His research materials for *Damnation*, collected at the Library of Congress, include several clippings from contemporary periodicals detailing Mendel's work.

16. See chapters 3, 7, and 10 of Higham, *Strangers*, for accounts of the periodic resurgence of these particular strands.

17. The third was the racial aspect.

18. Higham argues that the American Protective Association (APA)—a Protestant nativist organization dedicated to driving Catholics from political positions—grew rapidly in membership during the early years of the 1890s and spread especially quickly in the Midwest under the leadership of Henry F. Bowers. Much of the force behind it had dissipated by the middle of 1894 (*Strangers* 80–81).

19. See the work of Gossett, Horsman, and Knobel. Although Knox was English, his writing was widely circulated in the United States. Knobel claims that the association of "Paddy" with racial difference "left an unhappy legacy, for it had helped circulate very widely certain ideas about the centrality of 'blood' or peoplehood to nationality" (181).

20. See Roediger, *The Wages of Whiteness*, and Ignatiev, *How the Irish Became White*, for analyses of the Irish as a racialized group.

21. Horsman, chapter 4, "Racial Anglo-Saxonism in England," and Gosset, *Race*, contain descriptions of this ideology's elaboration and dissemination.

22. The essay is part of Frederic's collected papers in the Library of Congress. I could find no evidence of its publication.

23. Theron's nervousness is partly attested to by his oratorical gifts. As George Beard pointed out, "The masters in the oratorical art are always nervous. . . . delicacy of organization, united with Saxon force, makes America a nation of orators" ("English and American Physique" 595)

24. See Tom Lutz, *American Nervousness*, for a comprehensive description of the various treatments prescribed for neurasthenia.

Chapter 2: Flouting the Racial Border

1. See David Ward, *Poverty, Ethnicity, and the American City*, especially chapter 2. The tendency of nativist rhetoric to construct the slum as a proliferating wilderness within the heart of the civilized city, and depict the immigrant as an intractable savage dwelling within it, was an extension and reworking of earlier, sensationalist descriptions of city slums. As Ward points out (chapter 2), such descriptions appeared with increasing frequency from 1870 on, associating these nether regions with disease, vice, and debauchery. Within nativists' texts, the moral disorder conventionally associated with the city's slum regions became a function of those areas' foreign inhabitants.

NOTES TO PAGES 37–44

2. William Boelhower maintains that, for Americans, "both the issue of national dwelling and that of creating a homogeneous cultural identity opened up a preeminently spatial problematics" (10–11). Arguing that eliminating the Indian (and imposing the global space of the European onto the local space of the Indian) was the founding moment of the American polity, he further contends that from its inception the idea of the American nation was associated with the notion of space in its relation to race.

3. See, for example, Walker, "The Restriction of Immigration" and "Immigration and Degradation." For a comprehensive account of the various publications and forums in which nativists placed their work, see Higham, *Strangers*, 95 passim.

4. The term *germ plasm* was used by Charles Davenport, the intellectual leader of the American eugenic movement.

5. See McCann's discussion of this text in *Birth Control Politics in the United States*, on which I draw in this paragraph.

6. See Ripley, "Races in the United States," and Walker, "Immigration and Degradation," for further contemporary commentary on the inverse relation between foreign immigration and native fertility. The term *degenerate* was used with increasing frequency by scientists and social commentators in the latter half of the nineteenth century. Its precise meaning shifted, but, as Daniel Pick points out in his study of the discourses of degeneracy, "Degeneration became indeed the condition of conditions, the ultimate signifier of pathology. . . . It suggested at once a technical diagnosis and a racial prophecy" (8).

7. See Laura Hapke, *Girls Who Went Wrong*, for a discussion of the imaginative literature spawned by prostitution and the national crusade against the "social evil."

8. Feldman cites one such survey that was carried out by Katherine Bement Davis, superintendent of the State Reformatory for Women at Bedford Hills, New York. It "concluded that American-born women contributed overwhelmingly more than their proportion to New York prostitution" (199).

9. See Feldman for a discussion of the ways in which nativist and progressive attitudes to the issue of alien prostitution dovetailed.

10. Jenks and Lauk (313 passim) include the full text of these laws in *The Immigration Problem*.

11. See Bower on Frank Norris's fiction; she also emphasizes the popular association of prostitution with new immigration and demonstrates its influence on Norris's *Vandover and the Brute*.

12. The "continental model" referred to in the report was devised by A. J. B. Parent-Duchatelet, whose study of twelve thousand French prostitutes was published in 1836. The report, as Abigail Solomon-Godeau points out, "provided the model not only for fifty years of French reglementary systems, but also for British laws and investigations" (101). In this system, prostitutes were registered with police, confined to particular areas of the city, and subjected to regular medical checks for venereal diseases.

13. I take the term *racial border* from Abdul JanMohamed; see "Sexuality on/of the Racial Border."

14. These include going so far as to impersonate a tramp in order to spend a night in a flophouse. The result was "An Experiment in Misery," published in 1894 (Benfey 60).

15. Crane's father was a Methodist minister, and Crane attended one of Riis's lectures on the Jersey shore while a teenager (Benfey 59).

16. Accordingly, Benfey links the novel's preoccupation with maternal figures and infants to the fact that Crane had recently lost his mother (chapter 3, esp. 72).

17. June Howard's brilliantly incisive discussion of the use of perspective and the role of the reader/narrator-as-spectator in realist and naturalist fiction has been formative in my analysis of the role of boundaries and their transgression in Crane's novel. See *Form and History in American Literary Naturalism,* particularly chapter 4.

18. *Maggie* has also benefited from the renewed critical interest in naturalist fiction, specifically from a concern with the relation of this genre to the emergent culture of consumption. Mark Seltzer compares the representation of Maggie's mother with Jacob Riis's photographic depictions of maternal figures (*How the Other Half Lives*). Seltzer has observed that the recurrence of the maternal body in realist and naturalist fiction is a function, in part, of the wide circulation within turn-of-the-century American culture of a double discourse that he terms the "body-machine" complex. What must be noted, however, is the fact that the maternal figure in Crane's (and Riis's) text is also an immigrant figure. The anxiety and opprobrium elicited by the figure of the immigrant mother and her daughter in Crane's text must be traced in large measure to the nativist contribution to the immigration debate.

19. Sean Wilentz argues that by mid-century the Bowery had become the workers' Broadway, complete with "groggeries, oyster houses, dance halls, gambling dens and bordellos that catered to workingmen and adventuresome tourists" (257). Maggie frequents these leisure sites, as well as the theaters that characterized the region, in the latter half of the novel. The Bowery was thus a very different area than the much more indigent Five Points district. To middle-class observers such as Crane, however, the distinction between the two areas must have appeared minimal; both were replete with squalor and amorality (Ward, *Poverty* 43).

20. The nativists' construction of the Republic as a space under siege from immigrant hordes, as well as their anxiety over national and bodily pollution, have paranoiac elements. As outlined by Freud, paranoia is predicated on the construction of separate spheres and animated by the need to keep them separate. In Freud's account of paranoia, "Anything perceived as noxious within the ego . . . is then projected onto external objects: the 'subject' thus endows the external world with what it takes to be its own worst tendencies and qualities" (Smith, *Discerning* 95). By expelling all that is unwholesome and projecting it onto the figure of the other, a "fictional delusion" of a subject's "goodness and plenitude" can be maintained (96). Victor Burgin has linked paranoia with racism and nationalism: "I have begun to look at nationalism, at racism *as if* they might indeed be paranoid structures" (73, emphasis in the original).

21. Seltzer also points to the fact that the slums are "embodied in the body of a monstrously productive mother" (100).

22. See Berlant's description of the nature and function of the Statue of Liberty within what she dubs the "National Symbolic." Berlant describes the appearance of the latter as fetishistic—"indivisible" and "unperforated by 'gaps' or 'protrusions'" (23).

23. Walter Benn Michaels's argument is summarized in chapter 1. He contends that in the wake of *Plessy* vs. *Ferguson,* racial difference became relocated from physical features to character traits. Race became, he argues, a matter of internal essence. The attempt to establish the racial other as such drew heavily on the idea of hidden degeneracy. Michaels, "The Souls of White Folk."

24. As Riis put it, "'I am well persuaded . . . that half of the drunkenness that makes so many homes miserable is at least encouraged, if not directly caused, by the mismanagement and bad cooking at home'" (in Lubove 75).

25. As this characterization of the heroine suggests, *Maggie* belongs to the seduction genre, a form whose U.S. lineage dates back to the inception of the American novel. Intriguingly, Nancy Armstrong has argued that the sentimental novel, along with its closely related cousin the seduction novel, has always been centrally concerned with the national problem of racial identity. In "Why Daughters Die" she brilliantly expounds upon what she perceives to be the "racial logic" of the American variant of the genre. She demonstrates that Susanna Rowson's *Charlotte Temple* (1794) explores what would remain the chief preoccupation of this form throughout the nineteenth century: "How can English identity remain the same when it has to be reproduced outside of England?" (12). Armstrong also holds that sentimental and seduction novels' treatment of the issue is profoundly ambivalent. Within the space of a single text, readers can be offered both a biologically grounded answer to the question (in which case, a premium is placed on the daughter's sexual purity) and a culturally based response (in which case, the daughter's ability to reproduce an English household on foreign soil is prioritized). In both cases, however, the genre's concern to enact and maintain a racialized version of national identity leads it to "prefer . . . a dead daughter to an ethnically impure one" (12).

One might argue that Crane innovates on the seduction novel's racial logic in two respects. First, the daughter who transgresses and thus imperils ethnic purity is a racialized figure rather than a native one. Second, he definitively dispenses with the genre's traditional ambivalence concerning the origins of racial difference. Maggie's attempt to reproduce a normative (English) household in the ghetto by prettifying her grimy tenement dwelling does not redeem her for national belonging. She remains a racial interloper whose presence must be categorically expunged.

26. See Solomon-Godeau and Mulvey for discussions of the prostitute as a figure that bridges these divergent spaces. Mulvey argues that the underworld of prostitution is "the marginal area outside the ordered opposition between public and private, between consumption and production, between male and female" (70).

27. See Howard, *Form and History,* as well as Graff, "Metaphor and Metonymy." Graff argues that Crane sets up a rigid "binary opposition" between the two spaces of the novel. The tenement region and its exterior have analogues in the spaces occupied by the author/reader/middle-class, as opposed to that occupied by the underclass. By contrast, Howard's *Form and History* sees the impulse toward control as central to the structure and ideology of naturalist fiction, and it sees that impulse as an effect of naturalists' inability to maintain the rigid distinction between self and other. For Graff (434–45), Maggie is doomed because she is trapped inexorably in the underclass. My argument is closer to

that of Howard in that I see the porousness of the border as critical to the narrative's dynamics.

28. All nativist texts proclaim the need to reassert control over the space of the republican polity and over the integrity of the Anglo-Saxon body. In that respect, nativist texts are performative. Their exhaustive cataloging of the physical and mental differences of immigrants who are not Anglo-Saxon in order to produce a "scientific" taxonomy of racial types, their lengthy descriptions of the nature of the threat those aliens pose to the national health, and their assemblage of appendixes containing innumerable statistics pertaining to the new immigrants constitute a reassertion of distinction and hierarchy in the face of its seemingly imminent dissolution.

Chapter 3: President Roosevelt and Ellis Island

1. In *Primate Visions,* Donna Haraway has pointed to Roosevelt's iconic ability to augur the "regeneration of a miscellaneous, incoherent urban public threatened with genetic and social decadence, threatened with the prolific bodies of new immigrants" (29). See also Dyer, *President Roosevelt and the Idea of Race.*

2. A succinct discussion of Roosevelt's eugenic convictions can be found in Donald Pickens, *Eugenics and the Progressives.*

3. In "Race Decadence," Roosevelt pointed out that "the same racial crime is spreading almost as rapidly among the sons and daughters of immigrants as among the descendants of the native-born" (340).

4. Frank Warne wrote frequently on the topic of immigration; his work includes *The Slav Invasion and the Mine Workers* and *The Tide of Immigration.* He was secretary of the New York State Immigration Commission and also secretary of the Immigration Department of the National Civic Federation.

5. See Lears, "From Salvation to Self-Realization," as well as his book-length treatment of the same issue, *No Place of Grace.*

6. As Andrew Heinze states, "By the turn of the century. . . . consumption had come to be seen a sign of healthy 'ambition' for a higher standard of living. In the age of mass consumption, an attitude of resignation to a limited material existence appeared to be a problem. . . . [while] the conspicuous thrift of immigrants accustomed to scarcity posed a conflict with American ways" (30).

7. *The New Basis of Civilization* was based on a series of lectures in which Patten condensed as well as popularized the theories upon which he had been working since the late 1880s. As Daniel Fox explains in his introduction to the book, "Patten's efforts to relate the concept of abundance to the economic and scientific thought of his time are exemplified in three books written in the twenty years before the publication of *The New Basis: The Premises of Political Economy* (1887), *The Theory of Dynamic Economics* (1892), and *The Theory of Social Forces* (1896)."

8. Chase goes on to argue that McTeague is "the spiritual father of . . . Edgar Rice Burroughs's *Tarzan*" (191).

9. A berserker was a type of Norse warrior.

10. Hugh Dawson has discussed the fact that the name *McTeague* is Scotch-Irish, arguing that this, coupled with the fact that the name *Teague* was a common nickname for the Irish, lends credence to the argument that McTeague has immigrant roots. Norris's Norwegian heroine, Moran, also has an explicitly Irish name, however. In both cases the lack of fit between racial origin and surname suggests the presence of another of Norris's pervasive ironies.

11. Norris's obsession with racial extraction manifests itself in a need, across all his work, to ascribe racial origin to his non-native characters. Indeed, that origin is most often the first thing readers learn of them. Thus, Zerkow in *McTeague* is immediately presented as a "Polish Jew" (42), Maria Macapa is "the Mexican woman" (16), and Trina and her family are "Swiss-German." In the light of that meticulousness on Norris's part, the failure of the narrator to ascribe a racial or ethnic origin to McTeague is conspicuous. Even in the narrative flashback to his mining youth, which includes a description of his parents, no such ascription occurs. Furthermore, when McTeague returns at the end of the book to these mines, he is given an opportunity to assert his native status in a passage not attended by the narrator's otherwise almost pervasive irony: "'Are you a "cousin Jack [Cornishman]"?' asks the foreman. 'No. American'" avows McTeague (384).

Chapter 4: Sentimental Ambitions

1. In a sense, I will be using the term *Americanization* somewhat anachronistically, because the term did not achieve widespread currency until World War I. I follow Higham, however, in seeing the early work of Riis and others as linked to the later, full-blown Americanization movement. What ties the two forms of activism together is a belief in the social and cultural origin of racial difference, the idea that the alien was assimilable, and an urge to intervene in the lives of immigrants in order to facilitate that process.

2. In that report, *Changes in Bodily Form of Descendants of Immigrants,* Boas presented findings, based on a comparative study of the skull measurements of first- and second-generation immigrants, that identified culture and sociology rather than biology as paramount in the formation of racial differences: "In most of the European types that have been investigated the head form, which has always been considered one of the most stable and permanent characteristics of human races, undergoes far-reaching changes due to the transfer of the people from European to American soil. . . . We are compelled to conclude that when these features of the body change, the whole bodily and mental makeup of the immigrant may change. . . . Permanence of types in new surroundings appears rather as the exception than as the rule" (5).

3. Americanizers' methods of justifying intervention into tenements cannot be read apart from the larger backdrop of the growth of social sciences and the professions (particularly social work) that occurred in turn-of-the-century America. These developments were, as John Tagg has pointed out, intimately connected to the restructuring of the state during the same period. The new social sciences and professions "redefin[ed] the social as the object of their technical interventions," interventions that during the 1930s became important in "securing social regulation and consent within a social democratic frame-

work" (5, 10). Thus Kellor and Breckinridge's depiction of the immigrant as unable to carry out her maternal duties effectively in the New World also provides a powerful argument legitimizing, even demanding, state intervention. Gwendolyn Mink has illustrated how that intervention was made on the basis of culturalist and racist assumptions about normative gender roles.

4. George Sanchez discusses a similar focus among Americanizers on the West Coast who attempted to force the assimilation of Mexican families. "Motherhood," he argues, "in fact, became the juncture at which the Mexican immigrant woman's potential role in Americanization was most highly valued" (289).

5. Frances Kellor undertook graduate work in sociology at the University of Chicago although she left without taking a degree (Fitzpatrick 58). Her involvement in Progressive causes eventually led to her career as chief of New York State's Bureau of Industries and Immigration and later to her role as "close advisor to Theodore Roosevelt . . . member of the Progressive party's National Committee and head of the Bull Moose's innovative Progressive service" (Fitzpatrick 131). Higham discusses her participation in immigration issues in *Strangers*, 239 passim.

6. See the discussion of Katherine Anthony, *Mothers Who Must Earn*, in this chapter.

7. In both *Wages of Motherhood* and "The Lady and the Tramp," Gwendolyn Mink analyzes the convergence of racial and gender ideologies in middle-class women's reformist politics She argues cogently that "[reformers] made the imitation of a middle-class, Anglo American maternal ideal the price of woman's citizenship" (*Wages* 73). My argument is parallel to hers in that I, too, argue that different conceptions of the origin of racial difference marked off the nativist conceptualization of the immigrant problem from that of Americanizers. Similarly, she discusses the reformers' connection of "the problem of racial order to the material and cultural quality of motherhood. . . . the only way mothers from new races could produce ideal American democrats would be through reform and reward of maternal practice" ("Lady" 93). Mink's chief concern in the essay, however, is with the emergence of the American welfare state at the site of this complex of race and gendered assumptions. This chapter, by contrast, concerns itself with the debate over immigration itself being waged through and around the figure of the immigrant mother.

8. See Errol Lawrence, "Just Plain Common-Sense," for a discussion of how cultural racist discourse operated in Britain during 1970s and 1980s.

9. The exception here is the turn-of-the-century explosion of sentimental fiction written by and for African American women. See Claudia Tate, *Domestic Allegories of Political Desire*, for an account and analysis of this phenomenon.

10. Wexler's "Tender Violence" is an important and incisive account of sentimentalism's cultural work at the end of the nineteenth century with respect to these "marginal domestic populations" (18).

11. Philip Fisher (chapter 2, esp. 91 passim) sees this aspect of sentimentalism as constituting an expansive, democratic agenda.

12. As Wexler puts it, in Riis's slide-lantern shows the "consciousness of the social and

historical reciprocity of those who see and those who are seen is effaced precisely along the lines of deflection that sentimentality had entrenched" (37).

13. Similarly, Bonnie Thornton Dill indicates that "being a racial-ethnic woman in nine-teenth-century American society meant having. . . . a contradictory relationship to the norms and values about women that were being generated in the dominant white culture" (429). Glenn, however, drawing on the work of Phyllis Palmer, points out that the cult of domesticity created incompatible demands on white middle-class women, too. For example, the demand for cleanliness faced off against the ideal of purity and refinement. The contradiction was resolved by hiring racial ethnic women to perform such tasks, thereby "saving" middle-class white women for true womanhood ("From Servitude to Service Work" 8 passim).

14. The phrase "ways of seeing" is John Berger's.

15. In particular, see Stephanie Smith's discussion (*Conceived by Liberty*, chapter 2) of the construction of an American Madonna in *Women in the Nineteenth Century* by Margaret Fuller.

16. In *The Wages of Motherhood*, Mink argues (72 passim) that these reformers, whom she dubs "maternalists," liberalized race discourse while inscribing gender inequality in the newly emergent welfare state. My argument is that the articulation of cultural racism with a biologically rooted conception of gender difference, within the thinking of the Americanizers, helped reify racial difference no less solidly (although along a different axis) than the nativists' arguments.

17. See Stange's extended discussion of Riis's photographic practices in *Symbols of Ideal Life* (1–26). Stange also points out that Riis himself did not take many of the photographs that were used in his lectures and later cataloged as part of the Riis Collection. Of the 412 glass-plate negatives that constitute that collection, only about 250 are assumed to be taken by Riis. The others were collected from various sources, including newspaperwoman Jessie Tarbox Beals and amateur photographer Richard Hoe Lawrence.

18. A sketch by Kenyon Cox modeled on the photograph, rather than the photograph itself, was used in early editions of *How the Other Half Lives*.

19. For more on Riis's use of flash photography, see Maren Stange's discussion of his work (*Symbols of Ideal Life*, chapter 1).

20. He sees the division as instantiated both in documentary photography and across a range of different institutional contexts in this period, always invested in producing new forms of knowledge about the social body and new ways of exercising power over it.

21. Besides child-centeredness, the other two parts of the mother-script were "a new realm of feminine power" accrued through the mother-child relation and "a promise of fulfillment" pursuant to the association of womanhood and maternity (Theriot 26).

22. Sophonisba Breckinridge received a Ph.D. in political science from the University of Chicago and later earned a doctor of jurisprudence degree (Fitzpatrick 80 passim). She subsequently founded the School of Social Service Administration and became full professor there. I have drawn upon biographical accounts of Breckinridge, Kellor, and Edith Abbot in Fitzpatrick, *Endless Crusade*. The Breckinridge quotations are drawn from *New*

Homes for Old, volume 6 in the series on Americanization sponsored by the Carnegie Corporation.

23. Lillian Wald was trained as nurse and founded the Henry Street social settlement. *The House on Henry Street* is her account of her experiences therein.

24. This presentation of the white female as liberator of the benighted immigrant mother accords with a similar tradition in abolitionist literature. Jean Fagan Yellin has pointed out that many abolitionist texts present the "relationship between the passive female slave and the empowered white female liberator" (Nudelman 943 passim). See also Stephanie Smith's discussion of Stowe, who not only thematized the idea of suffering maternity in *Uncle Tom's Cabin* but also presented "her authorial destiny . . . as a sanctified mother" (94).

25. See Levenstein, *Revolution at the Table,* especially chapter 8, for a discussion of native attempts to influence immigrant foodways.

26. See Levenstein for an account of the attempt to develop methods for sterilizing milk in the face of massive child death rates in tenement areas. At the time Herzfeld was writing, the sterilization methods advocated by reformers proved so cumbersome that only upper- and middle-class families able to hire servants to carry out the process were able to implement them.

27. This depiction of the backward immigrant mother is one that many contemporary texts by immigrant daughters seem at pains to combat. See, for example, Anzia Yezierska's contrast between her savvy mother (a Russian Pole) and her naive immigrant father in the semiautobiographical *Bread Givers.*

Historians discussing the immigration of various ethnic groups have, by and large, reproduced this narrative of the assimilatory resistance of the "innately conservative" immigrant woman. In *Immigrant Women in the Land of Dollars* Elizabeth Ewen ponders the accuracy of reformers' description of the immigrant mother's backwardness, finally seeming to concur with it: "If immigrant mothers were consumed by the realities of home life, some of their daughters were quick to notice the new world. . . . While the mothers attempted to reassemble the terms of a known life, their daughters . . . step[ped] into the present" (67).

Some work stressing the central role the immigrant woman played in acculturating her family has begun to emerge, however. For example, in *Adapting to Abundance,* Andrew Heinze stresses consumption as a critical avenue to assimilation for Jewish immigrants at the turn of the century. A Jewish woman, as principal consumer for her family, was a key agent in forging the family's American identity. "Through her command over the household's consumers, the *baleboste* [housewife] initiated newcomers in the adoption of American ways. . . . and incorporated the demands of children for an American lifestyle" (114). Similarly, Ardis Cameron analyzes how immigrant women's twin tasks of child-rearing and wage labor coupled with the need to forge "strategies of survival translate[d] into 'street smart' concepts of life and labor" (57). She argues that in Lawrence, Massachusetts, "Women utilized the proximity of neighbors, friends, and kin to mutual advantage, socializing a variety of domestic tasks and customizing Old World principles of mutuality and collectivity. . . . Female collaborative activities, forged out of necessity, fostered networks that took root and strengthened. . . . Mutual dependence and coopera-tive assistance bound women together in a lattice-work of reciprocity" (60, 61).

28. In "The New Woman as Androgyne," Smith-Rosenberg maintains that new women such as Wald and Addams used "old arguments" concerning women's innate nurturing capacity to "justify public roles that, in their eyes, merely carried their 'mother's' ideas to a logical conclusion" (171).

29. In "Making Connections with the Camera," Stein argues that Riis's role as reformer of the aliens' physical context enabled him to move from the position of penniless im-migrant, to that of respected citizen, and eventually to confidante of Theodore Roosevelt.

30. William Ripley, too, had argued that "woman always is the conservative element in society" and pointed to "many thousand cases of destitution among foreign-born women . . . [whose] husband has outdistanced her in adaptation" ("Races" 750).

31. This is Higham's interpretation in *Strangers.*

Chapter 5: Eternal Mothers

1. Alexandra does not physically labor on her Nebraska farm. Her success lies in her investment skills combined with the adoption of up-to-date farming methods and tech-nology.

2. See Joseph Urgo, *Willa Cather and the Myth of American Migration,* for more on Alexandra's speculation, especially 46 passim.

3. See also *The Song of the Lark,* in which Cather similarly stresses the whiteness of her protagonist, Thea.

4. By contrast, the Bohemian Maria Shabata, a new immigrant, disrupts the Bergson's family relentless upward mobility. While Alexandra had invested her hopes in her brother Emil to "spring free of the soil," thereby completing the family's progress toward embourgeoisement, he succumbs instead to the charms of Maria. His consequent death at the hands of Maria's jealous husband foil Alexandra's plan. As the narrator puts it, Alexandra "blamed Maria bitterly" (173).

5. In an interview for the *New York Times* in 1924, Cather spoke of the Americanizing impulse with contempt: "Social workers, missionaries—call them what you will—go af-ter them, [immigrants] hound them, pursue them and devote their days and nights to-ward the great task of turning them into stupid replicas of smug American citizens. This passion for Americanizing everything and everybody is a deadly disease with us." Cather, *Willa Cather in Person,* 71–72.

6. See Stow Persons's discussion of Bourne and Kallen's views in *Ethnic Studies at Chicago,* 18–20.

7. Michaels argues in *Our America* that the capacity of cultural pluralism to elide its dependence on notions of race or blood renders it the modern form of nativism. Michaels's argument has been formative in my approach to cultural pluralism.

8. I borrow *racial domestication* from Jon Cruz, who discusses multiculturalism's "culturalist" bent as well as the links between that culturalism and global capitalism. In the contemporary conjuncture, he argues, "the ideology of privatization permeates the

reification of identity formations" (31). This "domestic(ated) pluralism" (35) is symptomatic of late capitalism in that "symbols and the busywork of social differentiation and distinction fill in where money and social institutions cannot" (31). Like Cruz, I employ the term *domestication* to gesture to the severing of identity from political and economic considerations. I use the term in one further sense: to convey the particular contours of the traits early cultural pluralists imputed to the new immigrants.

9. As Gordon and Newfield put it, culturalism can "shift attention from racialization to culture," thereby making "racism more difficult to acknowledge" (79).

10. Palmer, *Domesticity and Dirt*; Romero, *Maid in the U.S.A.*

11. Thus Randolph Bourne, for example, was not necessarily antirestrictionist. In "Trans-National America" he explains, "I do not mean that we shall necessarily glut ourselves with the raw product of humanity. It would be folly to absorb the nations faster than we could weave them. We have no duty either to admit or reject. It is purely a question of expediency" (262).

12. A lucid discussion of Kallen's pluralism appears in Higham, *Send These to Me* (203–8)

13. See Higham, *Strangers*, for a discussion of this provision of the bill. He argues that this was the beginning of "a nationalist attack on radicals" and that by 1919 there was a pervasive "impression that radicalism permeated the foreign-born population, that it flourished among immigrants generally and appealed to hardly anyone else" (227).

14. See Caroline Manning, *An Immigrant Woman and Her Job*, for accounts of such inequities experienced by immigrant women. As one such description runs, "One woman had been satisfied to take a job as a quiller upon the promise of getting weaving soon. When she saw that several new American girls were given weaving in preference to herself she began asking for looms also. . . . but she never did [attain one] . . . she left without understanding why she was not given a job as a weaver" (120).

In *Immigrant Acts*, Lisa Lowe makes a similar point about the racialization of immigrant labor in the context of a discussion of Chinese immigration policy in the United States in the 1880s. "Capital could increase profit and benefit from the presence of a racialized and tractable labor force up," she argues, "until the point at which the Chinese labor force grew large enough that it threatened capital accumulation by whites. At that point, by excluding and disenfranchising the Chinese in 1882, the state could constitute the 'whiteness' of the citizenry and granted political concessions to 'white' labor groups who were demanding immigration restrictions" (13).

15. San Juan has summarized the work of Robert Blauner: "Racial minorities . . . given the specific modes of their historical incorporation into the U.S. polity, have uninterruptedly produced their own authentic cultures of resistance in the process of life-and-death struggle. This epic of lived experience incarnated in cultural forms registers class and gender exploitation in the modality of racial oppression. But the power of this achievement is neutralized by the liberal consensus and inventoried as merely one specimen of ethnic diversity" (39).

16. Gordon and Newfield explore multiculturalism's roots in the cultural pluralism of Kallen and others. Although critiquing Kallen's "assumption that American capitalism

was not subject to the diversity principle and would foster the economic mobility required to integrate ethnic groups," they see his pluralism as an attack on assimilationism and his work as the welcome adumbration of "a *multicentered* national culture" (86).

17. See, for example, Randolph Bourne, "What Is Exploitation?" For a discussion of Fannie Hurst's involvement in progressive causes, see Abe Ravitz, *Imitations of Life*. He points out that Hurst's name was "prominently linked with that of Eleanor Roosevelt as both sought to draw attention to and to improve the situation of domestic workers" (30).

18. A resistance to modernization "fuel[s] the work of many modernists and make[s] them turn their imaginations . . . to the alternate space of the primitive" (Torgovnick 192). For cultural pluralists, that primitive space was identified with the communities of recently arrived immigrants.

19. Addams's essay "Immigration" was originally printed in *The Commons* in 1905.

20. For a particularly explicit example of a text that confuses heritage, practices, and traits, see W. I. Thomas, *Old World Traits Transplanted*. Although its title uses the word *traits*, the first chapter is entitled "Immigrant Heritages." The text uses the two signifiers interchangeably.

21. For Mrs. Bergson, too, "preserving was almost a mania" (17), but that interest renders her an anachronism within *O Pioneers!*

22. See John J. Murphy's discussion of Ántonia as earth mother in My Ántonia: *The Road Home*, 92 passim.

23. See Ravitz's summary in *Imitations of Life* of the critical reception to her work, which I draw upon in this paragraph.

24. Romero is summarizing the work of David Katzman's *Seven Days a Week*.

25. I borrow this felicitous formulation from Nancy Armstrong, *Desire and Domestic Fiction*, 75.

Conclusion

1. See Walter Benn Michaels, *Our America*, for an account of pluralism's congruence with nativist thought that proceeds along a different, albeit related, axis to my own. His account is specifically concerned with these discourses' common debt to essentialist versions of identity.

2. Among the recommendations of the Commission on Immigration Reform was the suggestion that employers be required to pay a special tax for each legal immigrant hired, to be used to create a reeducation fund for domestic workers.

3. See Dorothy Roberts, "Who May Give Birth to Citizens?" for an account of the position of the immigrant mother within the public debate on immigration.

4. See, for example, Marc Cooper, "The Heartland's Raw Deal," for the use of immigrant labor in the meat-packing industry in the Midwest. Periodic INS raids of the factories, coupled with the occasional deportation of illegal aliens found working there, helps keep the workforce docile and disinclined to agitate for the most basic labor rights.

Works Cited

Addams, Jane. "Immigration: A Field Neglected by the Scholar." In *Immigration and Americanization: Selected Readings,* comp. and ed. Philip Davis, 3–22. Boston: Ginn, 1920.

———. *Twenty Years at Hull House.* 1910. Reprint. New York: Macmillan, 1981.

"America's Challenge." *Time* Magazine 142 (Fall 1993): 3.

Ammons, Elizabeth. "Edith Wharton and Race." In *Cambridge Companion to Edith Wharton,* ed. Millicent Bell, 68–86. New York: Cambridge University Press, 1995.

Anthony, Katharine. *Mothers Who Must Earn.* New York: Survey Associates, 1914.

Appiah, Anthony Kwame. "Racisms." In *Anatomy of Racism,* ed. David Theo Goldberg, 3–17. Minneapolis: University of Minnesota Press, 1990.

Armstrong, Nancy. *Desire and Domestic Fiction: A Political History of the Novel.* New York: Oxford University Press, 1987.

———. "Why Daughters Die: The Racial Logic of American Sentimentalism." *Yale Journal of Criticism* 7, no. 2 (1994): 1–24.

Arnold, Matthew. *Culture and Anarchy: An Essay in Political and Social Criticism.* 1869. Reprint. New York: Macmillan, 1919.

Banta, Martha. *Imaging American Women: Idea and Ideals in Cultural History.* New York: Columbia University Press, 1987.

———. *Taylored Lives: Narrative Productions in the Age of Taylor, Veblen, and Ford.* Chicago: University Chicago Press, 1993.

Barker, Martin. *The New Racism: Conservatives and the Ideology of the Tribe.* Frederic: University Publications of America, 1982.

Barrett, Kate Waller. "The Immigrant Woman." In *Immigration and Americanization: Selected Readings,* ed. Philip Davis, 224–31. Boston: Ginn, 1920.

Beard, George M. *American Nervousness: Its Causes and Consequences; a Supplement to Nervous Exhaustion (Neurasthenia).* Introduction by Charles E. Rosenberg. 1881. Reprint. New York: Arno Press, 1972.

————. "English and American Physique." *North American Review.* 129 (1879): 588–603.

Bederman, Gail. *Manliness and Civilization: A Cultural History of Gender and Race in the United States, 1880–1917.* Chicago: University of Chicago Press, 1995.

Benedict, E. "A Bohemian Immigrant Mother." *The Survey,* Oct. 11, 1913, 56.

Benfey, Christopher. *The Double Life of Stephen Crane.* New York: Alfred A. Knopf, 1992.

Berger, John. *Ways of Seeing.* New York: Penguin, 1972.

Berlant, Lauren G. *The Anatomy of National Fantasy: Hawthorne, Utopia, and Everyday Life.* Chicago: University of Chicago Press, 1991.

Bhabha, Homi K. "The Other Question: The Stereotype and Colonial Discourse." *Screen* 24, no. 6 (1983): 18–36.

Boas, Franz. *Changes in Bodily Form of Descendants of Immigrants.* In *Reports of the Immigration Commission,* vol. 38. Washington: Government Printing Office, 1911.

Boelhower, William. *Through a Glass Darkly: Ethnic Semiosis in American Literature.* New York: Oxford University Press, 1987.

Bourne, Randolph. "Emerald Lake." In *The Radical Will: Selected Writings, 1911–1918,* selections and introduction by Olaf Hansen, 271–74. Preface by Christopher Lasch. New York: Urizen Books, 1977.

————. *The Radical Will: Selected Writings, 1911–1918,* selections and introduction by Olaf Hansen. Preface by Christopher Lasch. New York: Urizen Books, 1977.

————. "Trans-National America." In *The Radical Will: Selected Writings, 1911–1918,* selections and introduction by Olaf Hansen, 248–64. Preface by Christopher Lasch. New York: Urizen Books, 1977.

————. "What Is Exploitation?" In *The Radical Will: Selected Writings, 1911–1918,* selections and introduction by Olaf Hansen, 285–89. Preface by Christopher Lasch. New York: Urizen Books, 1977.

Bower, Stephanie. "Dangerous Liaisons: Prostitution, Disease, and Race in Frank Norris's Fiction." *Modern Fiction Studies* 42, no. 1 (1996): 31–60.

Bowlby, Rachel. *Just Looking: Consumer Culture in Dreiser, Gissing, and Zola.* New York: Methuen, 1985.

Brandt, John L. *Anglo-Saxon Supremacy; or, Race Contributions to Civilization.* Boston: Richard G. Badger, 1915.

Breckinridge, Sophinisba P. *New Homes for Old.* Introduction by William S. Bernard. 1921. Reprint. Montclair: Patterson Smith, 1971.

Brimelow, Peter. *Alien Nation: Common Sense about America's Immigration Disaster.* New York: Random House, 1995.

Brown, Gillian. *Domestic Individualism: Imagining Self in Nineteenth-Century America.* Berkeley: University of California Press, 1990.

Burgin, Victor. "Paranoiac Space." *New Formations* 12 (Winter 1990): 61–76.

Burr, Clinton Stoddard. *America's Race Heritage.* New York: National Historical Society, 1922.

Bushee, Frederick A. *Ethnic Factors in the Population of Boston.* 1903. Reprint. New York: Arno Press, 1970.

Cameron, Ardis. "Landscapes of Subterfuge: Working Class Neighborhoods and Immigrant Women." In *Gender, Class, Race, and Reform in the Progressive Era*, ed. Noralee Frankel and Nancy S. Dye, 56–72. Lexington: University Press of Kentucky, 1991.

Carby, Hazel V. *Reconstructing Womanhood: The Emergence of the Afro-American Woman Novelist.* New York: Oxford University Press, 1987.

———. "Schooling in Babylon." In *The Empire Strikes Back: Race and Racism in 1970s Britain*, 183–211. Centre for Contemporary Cultural Studies. London: Hutchinson, 1982.

Cardoso, Lawrence A. *Mexican Emigration to the United States, 1897–1931: Socio-Economic Patterns.* Tucson: University of Arizona Press, 1980.

Cather, Willa. *My Ántonia.* 1918. Reprint, with a foreword by Doris Grumbach. Boston: Houghton Mifflin, 1988.

———. *O Pioneers!* 1913. Reprint, with a foreword by Doris Grumbach. Boston: Houghton Mifflin, 1988.

———. *The Song of the Lark.* 1915. Reprint. New York: Bantam, 1981.

———. *Willa Cather in Person: Interviews, Speeches, and Letters.* Selected and edited by L. Brent Bohlke. Lincoln: University of Nebraska Press, 1986.

Chase, Richard V. *The American Novel and Its Tradition.* 1957. Reprint. New York: Gordian Press, 1978.

Chavez, Leo. R. "Immigration Reform and Nativism: The Nationalist Response to the Transnationalist Challenge." In *Immigrants Out! The New Nativism and the Anti-Immigrant Impulse in the United States*, ed. Juan F. Perea, 61–77. New York: New York University Press, 1997.

Cherniavsky, Eva. *That Pale Mother Rising: Sentimental Discourses and the Imitation of Motherhood in Nineteenth-Century America.* Bloomington: Indiana University Press 1995.

Committee on Foreign-Born Women of the Committee on Women in Industry of the Council of National Defense. "Making the Foreign Born One of Us." *The Survey*, May 25, 1918, 213–15.

Cooper, Marc. "The Heartland's Raw Deal: How Meat Packing Is Creating a New Immigrant Underclass." *The Nation*, Feb. 3, 1997, 11–16.

Cott, Nancy. *The Bonds of Womanhood: "Woman's Sphere" in New England, 1780–1835.* New Haven: Yale University Press, 1977.

Crane, Stephen. Maggie: A Girl of the Streets *and Other Short Fiction.* 1893. Reprint, with an introduction by Jayne Anne Phillips. New York: Bantam, 1988.

Cruz, Jon. "From Farce to Tragedy: Reflections on the Reification of Race at Century's End." In *Mapping Multiculturalism*, ed. Avery F. Gordon and Christopher Newfield, 19–39. Minneapolis: University of Minnesota Press, 1996.

Dawson, Hugh J. "McTeague as Ethnic Stereotype." *American Literary Realism* 20, no. 1 (1987): 34–44.

Dill, Bonnie Thornton. "Our Mother's Grief: Racial Ethnic Women and the Maintenance of Families." *Journal of Family History* 13, no. 4 (1988): 415–31.

Doyle, Laura. *Bordering on the Body: The Racial Matrix of Modern Fiction and Culture.* New York: Oxford University Press, 1994.

Dwight, Helen C. "The Immigrant Madonna, a Poem." *The Survey*, Dec. 11 1915, 281.

Dyer, Thomas G. *Theodore Roosevelt and the Idea of Race.* Baton Rouge: Louisiana State University Press, 1980.

Evans, Sara M. *Born for Liberty: A History of Women in America.* New York: Free Press, 1989.

Ewen, Elizabeth. *Immigrant Women in the Land of Dollars: Life and Culture on the Lower East Side, 1890–1925.* New York: Monthly Review Press, 1985.

Ewen, Stuart, and Elizabeth Ewen. *Channels of Desire: Mass Images and the Shaping of American Consciousness.* New York: McGraw Hill, 1982.

Fairchild, Henry Pratt. *Immigration: A World Movement and Its American Significance.* 1913. Reprint, rev. ed. New York: Macmillan, 1925.

———. *The Melting Pot Mistake.* 1926. Reprint. New York: Arno Press, 1977.

Feagin, Joe R. "Old Poison in New Bottles: The Deep Roots of Modern Nativism." In *Immigrants Out! The New Nativism and the Anti-Immigrant Impulse in the United States,* ed. Juan F. Perea, 13–43. New York: New York University Press, 1997.

Feeks, Dan. "Putting Mother in Her Right Place." *World Outlook* 4 (Oct. 1918): 9–10.

Feldman, Egal. "Prostitution, the Alien Woman and the Progressive Imagination, 1910–1915." *American Quarterly* 19 (Summer 1967): 192–206.

Fisher, Philip. *Hard Facts: Setting and Form in the American Novel.* New York: Oxford University Press, 1985.

Fitzpatrick, Ellen. *Endless Crusade: Women Social Scientists and Progressive Reform.* New York: Oxford University Press, 1990.

Foucault, Michel. *The History of Sexuality.* Vol. 1: *An Introduction.* Trans. Robert Hurley. New York: Vintage 1990.

Frederic, Harold. "Closing the Gates." In Collected Papers of Harold Frederic, Library of Congress, Washington, D.C.

———. *The Damnation of Theron Ware; or, Illumination.* 1896. Reprint, with an introduction by Scott Donaldson. New York: Penguin, 1986.

"From the Managing Editor." *Time* Magazine 142 (Fall 1993): 2.

Gardner, Jared. "What Blood Will Tell: Hereditary Determinism in *McTeague* and *Greed.*" *Texas Studies in Literature and Language* 36, no. 1 (1994): 51–74.

Giddings, Franklin H. "What Shall We Be? Comments on the Foregoing." *Century Magazine* 65 (March 1903): 690–92.

Giddings, Paula. "The Last Taboo." In *Race-ing Justice, En-gendering Power: Essays on Anita Hill, Clarence Thomas, and the Construction of Social Reality,* ed. and with an introduction by Toni Morrison, 441–70. New York: Pantheon Books, 1992.

Gilman, Sander L. "Black Bodies, White Bodies: Toward an Iconography of Female Sexuality in Late Nineteenth-Century Art, Medicine, and Literature." *Critical Inquiry* 12, no. 1 (1985): 204–42.

Gilroy, Paul. *"There Ain't No Black in the Union Jack": The Cultural Politics of Race and Nation.* Foreword by Houston A. Baker, Jr. Chicago: University Chicago Press, 1991.

Glenn, Evelyn Nakano. "From Servitude to Service Work: Historical Continuities in the Racial Division of Paid Reproductive Labor." *Signs* 18, no. 1 (1992): 1–43.

Goldberg, David Theo. "The Social Formation of Racist Discourse." In *Anatomy of Rac-*

ism, ed. David Theo Goldberg, 295–318. Minneapolis: University of Minnesota Press, 1990.

Goldman, Anne E. *Take My Word: Autobiographical Innovations of Ethnic American Working Women*. Berkeley: University of California Press, 1996.

Gordon, Avery F., and Christopher Newfield. "Multiculturalism's Unfinished Business," in *Mapping Multiculturalism*, ed. Avery F. Gordon and Christopher Newfield, 76–115. Minneapolis: University of Minnesota Press, 1996.

Gossett, Thomas F. *Race: The History of an Idea in America*. Dallas: Southern Methodist University Press, 1963.

Graff, Aida Farrag. "Metaphor and Metonymy: The Two Worlds of Crane's *Maggie*." *English Studies in Canada* 8, no. 4 (1982): 422–36.

Grant, Madison. *The Passing of the Great Race; or, The Racial Basis of European History*. 1916. 4th rev. ed., with prefaces by Henry Fairfield Osborn. New York: Charles Scribner's Sons, 1921.

Grant, Madison, and Charles Stewart Davidson, eds. *The Alien in Our Midst; or, "Selling Our Birthright for a Mess of Potage": The Written Views of a Number of Americans (Present and Former) on Immigration and Its Results*. New York: Galton Publishing, 1930.

Grimstead, David. *Melodrama Unveiled: American Theater and Culture, 1800–1850*. Chicago: University of Chicago Press, 1968.

Hapke, Laura. *Girls Who Went Wrong: Prostitutes in American Fiction, 1885–1917*. Bowling Green: Bowling Green State University Popular Press, 1989.

Haraway, Donna. "Teddy Bear Patriarchy: Taxidermy in the Garden of Eden, New York City, 1908–1936." In *Primate Visions: Gender, Race, and Nature in the World of Modern Science*, 26–58. New York: Routledge, 1989.

Harvey, David. *The Condition of Postmodernity: An Enquiry into the Origins of Cultural Change*. Cambridge: Blackwell Publishers, 1989.

Heinze, Andrew R. *Adapting to Abundance: Jewish Immigrants, Mass Consumption, and the Search for American Identity*. New York: Columbia University Press, 1990.

Herzfeld, Elsa. "Superstitions and Customs of the Tenement House Mother." *Charities* 14, no. 19 (1905): 983–86.

Higham, John. *Send These to Me: Immigrants in Urban America*. Rev. ed. Baltimore: Johns Hopkins University Press, 1984.

———. *Strangers in the Land: Patterns of American Nativism, 1860–1925*. New York: Atheneum Press, 1963.

Horsman, Reginald. *Race and Manifest Destiny: The Origins of American Racial Anglo-Saxonism*. Cambridge: Harvard University Press, 1981.

Horton, Isabelle. *The Burden of the City*. New York: Fleming H. Revell, 1904.

Howard, June. *Form and History in American Literary Naturalism*. Chapel Hill: University of North Carolina Press, 1985.

Howells, William Dean. "A Case in Point." In *Critical Essays on Frank Norris*, comp. Don Graham, 13–15. Boston: G. K. Hall, 1980.

"How to Develop American Sentiment among Immigrants." *Century Magazine* 40 (Jan. 1891): 471–73.

Hurst, Fanny. *Imitation of Life.* New York: P. F. Collier, 1933.

————. *Lummox.* 1923. Reprint. New York: Plume Books, 1989.

Ignatiev, Noel. *How the Irish Became White.* New York: Routledge, 1995.

Irving, Katrina. "Displacing Homosexuality: The Use of Ethnicity in Willa Cather's *My Ántonia.*" *Modern Fiction Studies* 36, no. 1 (1989): 91–103.

————. "Gendered Space, Racialized Space: Nativism, the Immigrant Woman, and Stephen Crane's *Maggie.*" *College Literature* 20, no. 3 (1993): 30–42.

Jameson, Fredric. *The Political Unconscious: Narrative as a Socially Symbolic Act.* Ithaca: Cornell University Press, 1981.

JanMohamed, Abdul R. "Sexuality on/of the Racial Border: Foucault, Wright, and the Articulation of 'Racialized Sexuality.'" In *Discourses of Sexuality: From Aristotle to AIDS,* ed. Domna Stanton, 94–116. Ann Arbor: University of Michigan Press, 1992.

Jenks, Jeremiah W., and W. Jett Lauck. *The Immigration Problem: A Study of American Immigration Conditions and Needs.* New York: Funk and Wagnalls, 1912.

Jewell, K. Sue. *From Mammy to Miss America and Beyond: Cultural Images and the Shaping of U.S. Social Policy.* New York, Routledge, 1993.

Kallen, Horace M. *Culture and Democracy in the United States: Studies in the Group Psychology of the American Peoples.* New York: Boni and Liveright, 1924.

————. "Democracy *versus* the Melting Pot." In *Culture and Democracy in the United States: Studies in the Group Psychology of the American Peoples,* 67–125. New York: Boni and Liveright, 1924.

Katzman, David. *Seven Days a Week: Women and Domestic Service in Industrializing America.* Urbana: University of Illinois Press, 1981.

Kellor, Frances. *Immigration and the Future.* New York: George H. Doran and Company, 1920.

————. "Neighborhood Americanization: A Discussion of the Alien in a New Country and of the Native American in His Home Country." Presented at the Colony Club, New York City, Feb. 8, 1918.

————. "Straight America." *Immigrants in America Review* 2 (July 1916): 9–25.

Kern, Stephen. *The Culture of Time and Space, 1880–1918.* Cambridge: Harvard University Press, 1983.

King, Miriam, and Steven Ruggles. "American Immigration, Fertility, and Race Suicide at the Turn of the Century." *Journal of Interdisciplinary History* 20, no. 3 (1990): 347–69.

Knobel, Dale T. *Paddy and the Republic: Ethnicity and Nationality in Antebellum America.* Middletown: Wesleyan University Press, 1986.

Laclau, Ernesto, and Chantal Mouffe. *Hegemony and Socialist Strategy: Toward a Radical Democratic Politics.* London: Verso, 1985.

Lawrence, Errol. "Just Plain Common Sense: The 'Roots' of Racism." In *The Empire Strikes Back: Race and Racism in 1970s Britain,* 47–94. Centre for Contemporary Cultural Studies. London: Hutchinson, 1982.

Lears, T. J. Jackson. *Fables of Abundance: A Cultural History of Advertising in America.* New York: Basic Books, 1994.

————. "From Salvation to Self-Realization: Advertising and the Therapeutic Roots of Consumer Culture, 1880–1930." In *The Culture of Consumption: Critical Essays in American History, 1880–1980,* ed. Richard Wightman Fox and T. J. Jackson Lears, 1–38. New York: Pantheon, 1983.

————. *No Place of Grace: Antimodernism and the Transformation of American Culture, 1880–1920.* New York: Pantheon Books, 1981.

Levenstein, Harvey. *Revolution at the Table: The Transformation of the American Diet.* New York: Oxford University Press, 1988.

Lowe, Lisa. *Immigrant Acts: On Asian American Cultural Politics.* Durham: Duke University Press, 1996.

Lubiano, Wahneema. "Black Ladies, Welfare Queens, and State Minstrels: Ideological War by Narrative Means." In *Race-ing Justice, En-gendering Power: Essays on Anita Hill, Clarence Thomas, and the Construction of Social Reality,* ed. and with an introduction by Toni Morrison, 323–63. New York: Pantheon Books, 1992.

Lubove, Roy. *The Progressives and the Slums: Tenement House Reform in New York City, 1890–1917.* Forewords by Samuel P. Hays and Philip S. Broughton. Westport: Greenwood Press, 1962.

Lutz, Tom. *American Nervousness, 1903: An Anecdotal History.* Ithaca: Cornell University Press, 1991.

MacFarlane, Lisa Watt. "Resurrecting Man: Desire and the Damnation of Theron Ware." *Studies in American Fiction* 20, no. 2 (1992): 127–44.

Manning, Caroline. *The Immigrant Woman and Her Job.* 1930. Reprint. New York: Arno Press, 1970.

Mayo-Smith, Richmond. *Emigration and Immigration: A Study in Social Science.* 1890. Reprint. New York: Charles Scribner's Sons, 1898.

Mayper, Joseph. "Americanizing Immigrant Homes." *Immigrants in America Review* 2, no. 2 (1916): 54–60.

McCann, Carole R. *Birth Control Politics in the United States, 1916–1945.* Ithaca: Cornell University Press, 1994.

McClintock, Anne. "'No Longer in a Future Heaven': Gender, Race and Nationalism." In *Dangerous Liaisons: Gender, Nation, and Postcolonial Perspectives,* ed. Anne McClintock, Aamir Mufti, and Ella Shohat for the Social Text Collective, 89–112. Minneapolis: University of Minnesota Press, 1997.

Merriman, Christina. "Old Country Mothers and American Daughters." *The Survey,* Oct. 25, 1913, 88.

Meyer, Stephen. *The Five Dollar Day: Labor Management and Social Control in the Ford Motor Company, 1908–1921.* Albany: SUNY Press, 1981.

Michaels, Walter Benn. *The Gold Standard and the Logic of Naturalism: American Literature at the Turn of the Century.* Berkeley: University of California Press, 1987.

————. *Our America: Nativism, Modernism, and Pluralism.* Durham: Duke University Press, 1995.

————. "The Souls of White Folk." In *Literature and the Body: Essays on Populations and Persons,* ed. Elaine Scarry, 185–209. Baltimore: John Hopkins University Press, 1988.

Michaud, Gustave. "What Shall We Be? The Coming Race in America." *Century Illustrated Monthly Magazine* 65 (March 1903): 683–90.

Miller, Madelaine Sweeny, and Gordon Thayer. "Two Poems of Motherhood." *The Survey,* Dec. 6, 1913, 244.

Mink, Gwendolyn. "The Lady and the Tramp: Gender, Race, and the Origins of the American Welfare State." In *Women, the State, and Welfare,* ed. Linda Gordon, 92–122. Madison: University of Wisconsin Press, 1990.

————. *The Wages of Motherhood: Inequality in the Welfare State 1917–1942.* Ithaca: Cornell University Press, 1995.

Morrison, Toni, ed. *Race-ing Justice, En-gendering Power: Essays on Anita Hill, Clarence Thomas, and the Construction of Social Reality.* Introduction by Toni Morrison. New York, Pantheon Books, 1992.

Morton, Patricia. *Disfigured Images: The Historical Assault on Afro-American Women.* New York: Greenwood Press, 1991.

Mulvey, Laura. "Melodrama Inside and Outside the Home." In *Visual and Other Pleasures,* 63–80. Bloomington: Indiana University Press, 1989.

Murphy, John J. My Ántonia: *The Road Home.* Boston: Twayne, 1989.

Myers, Robert. *Reluctant Expatriate: The Life of Harold Frederic.* Westport: Greenwood Press, 1995.

Nearing, Scott, and Nellie M. S. Nearing. *Woman and Social Progress: A Discussion of the Biologic, Domestic, Industrial and Social Possibilities of American Women.* New York: Macmillan, 1912.

Nelson, Brent A. *America Balkanized: Immigration's Challenge to Government.* Monterey, Va.: American Immigration Control Foundation, 1994.

Nelson, Dana. *The Word in Black and White: Reading "Race" in American Literature, 1638–1867.* New York: Oxford University Press, 1992.

Norris, Frank. "After Strange Gods." In *Collected Writings,* vol. 10, 189–98. Introduction by Charles G. Norris. Port Washington: Kennikat Press, 1967.

————. "A Case for Lombroso." In *Collected Writings,* vol. 10, 35–43. Introduction by Charles G. Norris. Port Washington: Kennikat Press, 1967.

————. *McTeague: A Story of San Francisco.* 1899. Reprint, ed. and with an introduction by Kevin Starr. New York: Penguin, 1982.

————. *Moran of the* Lady Letty: *A Story of Adventure off the California Coast.* 1898. Reprint. New York: AMS Press, 1971.

Nudelman, Franny. "Harriet Jacobs and the Sentimental Politics of Female Suffering." *ELH* 59 (Winter 1992): 939–64.

Painter, Nell. "Hill, Thomas, and the Power of Racial Stereotype." In *Race-ing Justice, En-gendering Power: Essays on Anita Hill, Clarence Thomas, and the Construction of Social Reality,* ed. and with an introduction by Toni Morrison, 200–214. New York: Pantheon Books, 1992.

Palmer, Phyllis. *Domesticity and Dirt: Housewives and Domestic Servants in the United States, 1920–1945.* Philadelphia: Temple University Press, 1989.

Patten, Simon N. *The New Basis of Civilization.* 1907. Reprint, ed. and with an introduction by Daniel Fox. Cambridge: Harvard University Press, 1968.

Pehotsky, Bessie Olga. *The Slavic Immigrant Woman.* 1925. Reprint. San Francisco: R and E Research Associates, 1970.

Perea, Juan F., ed. *Immigrants Out! The New Nativism and the Anti-Immigrant Impulse in the United States.* New York: New York University Press, 1997.

Persons, Stow. *Ethnic Studies at Chicago, 1905–1945.* Urbana: University of Illinois Press, 1987.

Pick, Daniel. *Faces of Degeneration: A European Disorder, c. 1848–c. 1918.* New York: Cambridge University Press, 1989.

Pickens, Donald K. *Eugenics and the Progressives.* Nashville: Vanderbilt University Press, 1968.

Popenoe, Paul. "The Immigrant Tide." In *The Alien in Our Midst; or, "Selling Our Birthright for a Mess of Pottage,"* ed. Madison Grant and Charles Stewart Davidson, 210–13. New York: Galton Publishing, 1930.

Radhakrishnan, Rajagopalan. "Nationalism, Gender, and the Narrative of Identity." In *Nationalisms and Sexualities,* ed. Andrew Parker et al., 77–95. New York: Routledge, 1992.

———. "Postmodernism and the Rest of the World." *Journal of Social Organization* 1, no. 2 (1994): 305–40.

Ravitz, Abe. *Imitations of Life: Fannie Hurst's Gaslight Sonatas.* Carbondale: Southern Illinois University Press, 1997.

"Rebirth of a Nation, Computer-Style." *Time* magazine 142 (Fall 1993): 66–67.

Richardson, Bertha June. *The Woman Who Spends, a Study of Her Economic Function.* Introduction by Ellen H. Richards. Boston: Whitcomb and Barrows, 1910.

Ripley, William Z. "Races in the United States." *Atlantic Monthly* 102 (Nov. 1908): 745–59.

———. *The Races of Europe: A Sociological Study.* New York: D. Appleton, 1899.

Riis, Jacob. *The Battle with the Slum.* 1901. Reprint. New York: Macmillan, 1902.

———. *How the Other Half Lives: Studies among the Tenements of New York.* 1901. Reprint, with a preface by Charles A. Madison. New York: Dover Publications, 1971.

———. *The Peril and the Preservation of the Home.* Philadelphia: George W. Jacobs, 1903.

Roberts, Diane. *The Myth of Aunt Jemima: Representations of Race and Region.* London: Routledge, 1994.

Roberts, Dorothy E. "Who May Give Birth to Citizens? Reproduction, Eugenics and Immigration." In *Immigrants Out! The New Nativism and the Anti-Immigrant Impulse in the United States,* ed. Juan F. Perea, 205–19. New York: New York University Press, 1997.

Roediger, David R. *The Wages of Whiteness: Race and the Making of the American Working Class.* London: Verso, 1991.

Rogin, Michael. *Blackface, White Noise: Jewish Immigrants in the Hollywood Melting Pot.* Berkeley: University of California Press, 1996.

Romero, Mary. *Maid in the U.S.A.* New York: Routledge, 1992.

Roosevelt, Theodore. "Race Decadence." In *Theodore Roosevelt: An American Mind. A Selection from His Writings,* ed. and with an introduction by Mario R. DiNunzio, 339–43. New York: Penguin, 1995.

————. *Theodore Roosevelt: An American Mind: A Selection from His Writings.* Ed. and with an introduction by Mario R. DiNunzio. New York: Penguin, 1995.

Ross, Edward Alsworth. *The Old World in the New: The Significance of Past and Present Immigration to the American People.* 1914. Reprint. New York: Jerome Ozer, 1971.

Rossiter, W. S. "The Diminishing Increase of Population." *Atlantic Monthly* 88 (Aug. 1901): 212–19.

Royce, Samuel. *Deterioration and Race Education with Practical Application to the Condition of the People and Industry.* New York: Edward O. Jenkins, 1878.

Russo, Mary J. *The Female Grotesque: Risk, Excess, and Modernity.* New York: Routledge, 1995.

————. "Female Grotesques: Carnival and Theory." In *Feminist Studies, Critical Studies,* ed. Teresa de Lauretis, 213–29. Bloomington: Indiana University Press, 1986.

Ryan, Mary. *Empire of the Mother: American Writing about Domesticity, 1830 to 1860.* New York: Institute for Research in History and Haworth Press, 1982.

Sanchez, George J. " 'Go After the Women': Americanization and the Mexican Immigrant Woman, 1915–1929." In *Unequal Sisters: A Multi-Cultural Reader in U.S. Women's History,* ed. Ellen Carol Dubois and Vicki L. Ruiz, 284–97. 2d ed. New York: Routledge, 1994.

Sangster, Margaret. *Radiant Motherhood: A Book for the Twentieth- Century Mother.* Indianapolis: Bobbs-Merrill, 1905.

San Juan, E., Jr. *Racial Formations/Critical Transformations: Articulations of Power in Ethnic and Racial Studies in the United States.* New Jersey, Humanities Press, 1992.

Seltzer, Mark. *Bodies and Machines.* New York: Routledge, 1992.

Shaler, N. S. "European Peasants as Immigrants." *Atlantic Monthly* 71 (May 1893): 646–55.

Shi, David E. *Facing Facts: Realism in American Thought and Culture, 1850–1920.* New York: Oxford University Press, 1995.

Sinclair, Upton. *The Jungle.* 1906. New York: Signet, 1960.

Sklar, Martin J. *The Corporate Reconstruction of American Capitalism, 1890–1916: The Market, the Law, and Politics.* New York: Cambridge University Press, 1988.

Smith, Paul. *Discerning the Subject.* Minneapolis: University of Minnesota Press, 1988.

Smith, Stephanie. *Conceived by Liberty: Maternal Figures and Nineteenth-Century American Literature.* Ithaca: Cornell University Press, 1994.

Smith-Rosenberg, Carroll. *Disorderly Conduct: Visions of Gender in Victorian America.* New York: Alfred A. Knopf, 1985.

————. "The New Woman as Androgyne: Social Disorder and Gender Crisis, 1870–1930." In *Disorderly Conduct: Visions of Gender in Victorian America,* 245–96. New York: Alfred A. Knopf, 1985.

Solomon-Godeau, Abigail. "The Legs of the Countess." *October* 39–40 (Winter 1986): 65–108.

Speek, Peter A. *A Stake in the Land.* 1921. Reprint, with an introduction by Rabel J. Burdge and Everett M. Rogers. Montclair: Patterson Smith, 1971.

Spillers, Hortense J. "Mama's Baby, Papa's Maybe: An American Grammar Book." *Diacritics: A Review of Contemporary Criticism* 17 (Summer 1987): 65–81.

Stange, Maren. *Symbols of Ideal Life: Social Documentary Photography in America, 1890–1950.* New York: Cambridge University Press, 1989.

Stansell, Christine. *City of Women: Sex and Class in New York, 1789–1860.* New York: Alfred A. Knopf, 1986.

———. "White Feminists and Black Realities: The Politics of Authenticity." In *Race-ing Justice, En-gendering Power: Essays on Anita Hill, Clarence Thomas, and the Construction of Social Reality,* ed. and with an introduction by Toni Morrison, 251–68. New York, Pantheon Books, 1992.

Stein, Sally. "Making Connections with the Camera: Photography and Social Mobility in the Career of Jacob Riis." *AfterImage* 10 (May 1983): 9–16.

Steinberg, Stephen. *The Ethnic Myth: Race, Ethnicity and Class in America.* Boston: Beacon Press, 1989.

Stella, Joseph. "The Immigrant Madonna" [cover]. *The Survey,* Dec. 1, 1922.

Stepans, Nancy Ley. "Race and Gender: The Role of Analogy in Science." In *Anatomy of Racism,* ed. David Theo Goldberg, 38–57. Minneapolis: University of Minnesota Press, 1990.

Stoddard, Lothrop. *The Rising Tide of Color against White World Supremacy.* Introduction by Madison Grant. New York: Scribner's, 1920.

Strong, Josiah. *The Challenge of the City.* New York, Young People's Missionary Movement, 1907.

———. *Our Country: Its Possible Future and Its Present Crisis,* ed. Jurgen Herbst. 1886. Reprint. Cambridge: Harvard University Press, 1963.

Szasz, Ferenc M., and Ralph H. Bogardus. "The Camera and the American Social Conscience: The Documentary Photography of Jacob A. Riis." *New York History* 55, no. 4 (1974): 409–36.

Tagg, John. *The Burden of Representation: Essays on Photographies and Histories.* Amherst: University of Massachusetts Press, 1988.

Tate, Claudia. *Domestic Allegories of Political Desire: The Black Heroine's Text at the Turn of the Century.* New York: Oxford University Press, 1992.

Theriot, Nancy M. *The Biosocial Construction of Femininity: Mothers and Daughters in Nineteenth-Century America.* New York: Greenwood Press, 1988.

Thomas, William I., with Robert E. Park and Herbert A. Miller. *Old World Traits Transplanted.* 1921. Reprint, with an introduction by Donald R. Young. Montclair: Patterson Smith, 1971.

Tompkins, Jane. *Sensational Designs: The Cultural Work of American Fiction, 1790–1860.* New York: Oxford University Press, 1985.

Torgovnick, Marianna. *Gone Primitive: Savage Intellects, Modern Lives.* Chicago: University of Chicago Press, 1990.

True, Ruth. *The Neglected Girl.* New York: Survey Associates, 1914.

United States Immigration Commission. *Abstracts of Reports of the Immigration Commission, with Conclusions and Recommendations and Views of the Minority.* Vols. 1 and 2. Washington, D.C.: Government Printing Office, 1911.

———. *The Fecundity of Immigrant Women.* In *Reports of the Immigration Commission,* Vol. 28. Washington, D.C.: Government Printing Office, 1911.

Urgo, Joseph R. *Willa Cather and the Myth of American Migration*. Urbana: University of Illinois Press, 1995.

Vice Commission of the City of Chicago. *The Social Evil in Chicago: A Study of Existing Conditions, with Recommendations by the Vice Commission of Chicago*. Chicago: Gunthrop Warren Printing, 1911.

Wald, Lillian D. *The House on Henry Street*. 1915. Reprint, with an introduction by Eleanor L. Brilliant. New Brunswick: Transaction Publishers, 1990.

Wald, Priscilla. *Constituting Americans: Cultural Anxiety and Narrative Form*. Durham: Duke University Press, 1995.

Walker, Francis A. "Immigration and Degradation." *The Forum* 11 (Aug. 1891): 634–44.

———. "The Restriction of Immigration." *Atlantic Monthly* 77 (June 1896): 822–29.

Ward, David. *Poverty, Ethnicity, and the American City, 1840–1925: Changing Conceptions of the Slum and the Ghetto*. New York: Cambridge University Press, 1989.

Ward, Robert DeCourcy. "National Eugenics in Relation to Immigration." *North American Review* 192, no. 1 (1910): 56–68.

Warne, Frank Julian *The Immigrant Invasion*. New York: Dodd, Mead, 1913.

———. *The Slav Invasion and the Mine Workers: A Study in Immigration*. Philadelphia: J. B. Lippincott, 1904.

———. *The Tide of Immigration*. New York: D. Appleton, 1916.

"A Western Realist." *Washington Times*, April 23, 1899. Reprinted in *Frank Norris: The Critical Reception*, ed. Joseph McElrath, Jr., and Katherine Knight, 46–49. New York: Burt Franklin, 1981.

Wexler, Laura. "Tender Violence: Literary Eavesdropping, Domestic Fiction and Educational Reform." In *The Culture of Sentiment: Race, Gender, and Sentimentality in Nineteenth-Century America*, ed. Shirley Samuels, 9–38. New York: Oxford University Press, 1992.

Wharton, Edith. *The House of Mirth*. 1905. Reprint, with an introduction by Cynthia Griffin Wolff. New York: Penguin, 1985.

Wilentz, Sean. *Chants Democratic: New York City and the Rise of the American Working Class, 1788–1850*. New York: Oxford University Press, 1984.

Williams, Raymond. *Marxism and Literature*. New York: Oxford University Press, 1977.

Yezierska, Anzia. *Bread Givers: A Novel: A Struggle between a Father of the Old World and a Daughter of the New*. 1925. Reprint, with an introduction by Alice Kessler Harris. New York: Persea Books 1975.

Zaborowska, Magdalena J. *How We Found America: Reading Gender through East European Immigrant Narratives*. Chapel Hill: University of North Carolina Press, 1995.

Index

KATRINA IRVING is an associate professor of English at George Mason University, where she also teaches in the cultural studies doctoral program.

Typeset in 10/13 Minion
with Nofret display
Designed by Dennis Roberts
Composed by Jim Proefrock
at the University of Illinois Press
Manufactured by Thomson-Shore, Inc.

University of Illinois Press
1325 South Oak Street
Champaign, IL 61820-6903
www.press.uillinois.edu